This book is dedicated to my husband Chris, the miracle man himself. You are my best friend and partner for life. Without you, there would be no story. You are the life of our family and my hero. When I grow up, I want to be just like you. To my kids who were our rock. You are such troopers to go through what you did and still keep it together. Thank you to you and Mom for pushing me to work on this book. To our extended family who have supported us through all the hard stuff. To the many friends who helped us on our journey toward healing. Your kindness never went unnoticed and you know who you are. To the ones who went to be with Jesus before us: Tammi, Scotty, Danny, Jeff, Bryce, Donavan, Michelle and others we met along the way. You are all warriors and we will see you again someday soon. To Jim and Sandi Morrison, true cancer warriors who led the way for us. To the Heart of the City Church in Coeur d'Alene for treating us like family from Day One. To Dr. Danko and the Seattle Cancer Care Alliance team for using science and grit to help save my husband. To the selfless, anonymous donor whose blood is now coursing through my husband's veins. Without you we might have had a completely different outcome. To my editor who gave me confidence that I could do this. Thank you for your encouragement when you could tell I was drowning. And to my Lord and Saviour Jesus Christ, who gives me the hope I need to press on, even in the darkest of days.

To: Lynsee
The hard times
just make the good
times sweeter
♡
Shelley

FOREWORD

My mother is quite the woman. As I write this, I can't help but smile thinking about her. She is selfless, God-fearing, generous and hard-working. She is the most beautiful woman in the world and she doesn't even know it. Her outside beauty is stunning, but her inside beauty is even more radiant. As a young girl, I watched helplessly while my father's body deteriorated from cancer. I saw my mother hold whatever was left together for the sake of her family. She took care of my father, not only as his wife, but as his caregiver and cheerleader. On top of this, she worked a full-time job trying to support us four children and pay my father's medical bills, all while we lived hundreds of miles from our home. I'm sure we kids didn't make it any easier. I'm honestly not sure how she held it together. Throughout this journey of literal blood, sweat and tears, my mother held onto God's promises. She wrote this book because she felt deeply that it would help someone else who was going through their own cancer journey. In this story, she shares how God held our family in the palms of His hands. Mom, your part of this journey has touched my life profoundly. I hope you know that I will always be your biggest fan. I love you with all my heart. —Joya Kennedy.

INTRODUCTION

In the middle of winter, 2013, my husband Chris received a devastating diagnosis that stopped our lives in their tracks and brought our family to its knees. It left us grasping at hope and searching desperately for answers. Gratefully, we knew how to run to God with our troubles. Throughout our cancer journey, my family and I witnessed God leading us step by step. It felt like the Bible story, a cloud by day and a pillar of fire by night, yet in His own unique and different way. Throughout all of our ups, downs and crazy challenges, God personally touched our family in ways far beyond coincidence. This is a story of hope. You need to have something to hang onto when you are about to hurdle off that cliff. Our family has walked through the fire of cancer, and come out the other side. My wish is that our story will help you find hope, faith, joy and peace, whether you are enduring a challenge in your life or helping and empathizing with someone else who is. God is in charge! He guides us on our most treacherous journeys. The next time life throws you a curveball, you will remember there is someone you can turn to for help. And be assured that good things always come out of that difficulty. Sometimes miraculous, wonderful things. This book tells it like it is, sharing our souls, offering the intimate, the painful, the funny and beautiful times along the cancer journey. It was difficult to relive some of these memories as I wrote. But if even one person is helped by telling our story, it will all be worth it.

UNDER THE WEATHER

"YOU DON'T KNOW WHAT YOU'VE GOT 'TIL IT'S GONE."

—JONI MITCHELL

It all started with a headache. We were at our son's basketball game and my husband Chris asked me to drive home. Mr. Type A never asked me to drive. It was wintertime and we figured it was the flu, so Chris took some Nyquil and went to bed to sleep it off.

He stayed in bed for five days.

Finally, on a Thursday afternoon I will never forget, just three weeks into 2013, our 11-year-old son Jared came to me.

"Daddy's got a bloody nose and has been throwing up blood," he said.

I felt an instant flood of guilt. It had been a busy week at work and home, and somehow I'd missed that Chris's supposed flu had taken a more dangerous turn.

Chris was one of those guys who never got sick and never went to the doctor. Once a Marine, always a Marine. "Pain is just weakness leaving the body" was a mantra I had heard for years.

In recent months, he had been feeling more tired than normal. We'd learned that his biological father, who he hadn't seen since a toddler, had died at 52 of a massive heart attack. So Chris had scheduled a recent physical at the local VA clinic himself. It was the first time I could remember in our married life that he had initiated a doctor visit. Previously, when the rest of us were battling different kinds of injuries such as herniated discs, broken bones, bladder problems or ear infections, he would give us a hard time about seeking medical intervention. In his mind, going to the doctor was a waste of money.

"They get paid to find something wrong with you." he would say. "They just need to make their boat payment."

Some of this approach came from his time in the Marine Corps, and some of it came from his adopted dad, a logger born in 1916 who was as tough as they come.

It was a source of many of our arguments. When one of our four very active children would get hurt, I would want to take them to the emergency room or urgent care center, and Chris would vehemently disagree. I usually won. Then the kids and I could gloat when the X-ray came back and showed a broken bone and one of them would come home in a cast.

"You were wrong again," I would tell my husband in a not-so-joking manner.

In typical mama bear fashion, when one of my kids is sick, there is no one and nothing that can stand in my way from getting them the help they need. Money is no object. Chris, on the other hand, is the practical one of us who is not run by his emotions. He would envision the $10,000 bill about to come his way. He used to tease me that if someone had a hangnail, I would call Life Flight.

At the VA, they'd run some blood work, given him an exam and a clean bill of health. Nothing out of the ordinary except his blood pressure was a little bit elevated, which can happen when a patient is stressed in the doctor's office. His white blood count was also a bit elevated. Not unusual, they said, since Chris felt like he was fighting off a cold or something.

Health insurance was another debate between us. My husband, being the cheapskate that he was, always refused the coverage.

"I'm a veteran. The VA will take care of me," he would say.

I never felt comfortable fully relying on the VA. I thought there were a lot of gray areas. I'd heard that the VA would only cover service-connected issues. Or that if the veteran ended up at the ER, it had better be a bona-fide emergency, or else the VA wouldn't cover it. Things like that.

So I had always pushed Chris to get him coverage through my work. Just so we had a backup plan. I already had coverage on myself and the kids. Eventually I'd worn him down. He agreed to the coverage and starting that January, he would now be covered on my health insurance policy, a policy with no spending cap. Little did we know at the time, that just three weeks after his coverage started the new health insurance policy would be an absolute Godsend.

Our last few years had been arduous ones. The real estate markets across America had corrected and we were one of those families who lost our home. We filed for bankruptcy and moved across the country for a fresh start and a more favorable place to raise our kids.

My husband was born to be an entrepreneur. His childhood and Marine Corps friends always teased him about the times he traded them out of their lunches, pencils and motorcycles. They would joke, "Is anything you own not for sale?" He had run small businesses, owned an RV park, opened a restaurant, worked in the car business and done multi-level marketing.

But this financial crisis, and the period that followed, had affected him to his core. He did not have the seed money to invest into a new venture. And he was tired of dragging his family through the ups and downs of small business ownership. He was frustrated that he had lost so much and was essentially starting over again at the age of 45. Some people might call his state of mind a mid-life crisis, except in his case it was different. Chris never wanted a new wife or bigger toys; he just wanted a way to provide for his family and leave a legacy. I knew his heart was always in the right place.

He never went off the deep end and had an affair, never bought that expensive convertible. That wasn't his style. He was loyal to his God, his wife and kids and friends above all else. And I knew he was grateful for our marriage and our four beautiful children. During this time of economic recession and personal reflection, his friends would confide in him about their lack of money, job loss or home loss and Chris would remind them. "We have our health, right? Our families are healthy and alive. Money comes and money goes. The greatest blessing is our health and family." He would remind them that there are billionaires who have been diagnosed with cancer who would give all the money they had to cure their disease and simply live.

Chris was always one of those glass-half-full people. You know the type. The kind of guy who never complains, and always finds the silver lining in every cloud. The former Marine in him takes what life gives him, bucks up and makes something good out of it. He has always been able to wake up in the morning with a song in his heart and seems to be able to look at the bright side of even the worst of circumstances. Even losing his mom at 17 had not dampened this outlook. Little did we know that his Pollyanna attitude was about to be tested once again. This time, it was personal.

THE PROPHECY

"NO PROPHECY EVER ORIGINATED FROM HUMANS. INSTEAD,
IT WAS GIVEN BY THE HOLY SPIRIT AS HUMANS SPOKE UNDER
GOD'S DIRECTION." —1 PETER 1:21

It was a wintery January afternoon in Coeur d'Alene, Idaho. We were hunkering down trying to stay warm, planning only to venture out to a sports bar to watch Chris's favorite football team, the Seahawks, who were finally in the playoffs after many losing seasons.

Our neighbors dropped in, inviting us to their church that evening for a special guest speaker. They had three towheaded little toddlers. We had grown extremely fond of their family, since they reminded us of our own four children, who by that point in our life ranged from ages 11 to 20. It seemed as if just yesterday our kids had been babies and it had gone by all too quickly. We relished their 4-year-old's unannounced visits. He would sneak away while his parents were sleeping and wander into our house, wearing his toddler wrestling singlet and his boots on the wrong feet. He would proudly announce, "Maddox is here and he's wearing his dinosaur boots!"

We didn't know much about the church event that night other than it was called The Sound. I grew up in a Charismatic Christian home, but my husband, who was raised as a Lutheran, would not normally have accepted this type of invitation. It was a church we were not familiar with and we had already made plans. To my surprise, he accepted. Maybe he assumed I would be just as likely to want to go to church as I would be to watch his beloved Seahawks, since I was a Denver Broncos fan. Ha!

So instead of watching the playoffs, we attended the first night of the church event. This was a big deal because his whole life he had been rooting for a team who usually lost. It turned out to be a prophecy conference, and the speaker was nothing like I had imagined. I didn't know what to expect from a modern-day prophet, but this man was an excellent speaker. He was middle-aged and well-dressed. He seemed so relatable and down to earth, while being funny and entertaining.

We watched with growing wonder as he did something he called, "reading people's mail." He personally addressed people in the congregation, including the neighbors who invited us and some of other other friends who happened to be there. It was almost like he could read their minds. He actually told one of the people that his birthday was April 6.

How does this man know those things? I wondered to myself. It was really remarkable to observe and we didn't know exactly what to make of it. After all, our neighbors were very low-profile people, and this man had just told everyone things about them that no one would know.

After the service, Chris ran into Wendy's to grab us some dinner. I sat in the car, talking to God. My prayer went something like this: *You know Lord, that you and I are tight. I'm okay if you don't speak to me through this prophet, but I greatly feel Chris desperately needs to hear from you. I'm begging you, God, please speak to my husband!*

I kept my prayer to myself as we ate our dinner. Out of the blue, Chris mentioned that he would like to go to the next service the following day. I agreed with a hopeful heart. *But what are the odds the prophet will pick us out of a church building full of people and speak to us?* I decided not to get my hopes too high.

The next morning we headed back to the church along with Jared, and our daughter, Joya, 17. On the way to church, we joked that maybe the prophet would talk to us and say something about a house. We had recently been looking at a house project; dreaming, really, because it was way over our housing budget. *If he mentions the house, we'll know it's 100 percent real. Of course this will never happen.*

As we walked into the sanctuary, my thoughts continued. *Where should we sit if we want him to talk to us?* Then I had to remind myself how ridiculous that was. If this man truly heard from God, I was pretty sure he could find us no matter where we sat. We found a seat and the service began.

The prophet's name was Tracy. He was as well-dressed, funny and entertaining as he'd been the night before. Tracy started out by preaching about faith. At the very end, he started prophesying to a few people. It was all very interesting to me. I was watching my kids and Chris to see how they were reacting, since this was all so new to us. At one point during the sermon, Chris had leaned over and whispered to me, "I really want to hear from God." Sometime after that, Tracy looked right at me and then said, "You in the pink sweater, I keep looking at you." Then he started telling another story to the congregation, and Chris again leaned over to me and whispered, "Are you ready? You better get ready!"

I wasn't sure if I was ready, but I knew Chris was ready to hear from God through this man.

A prophecy from a prophet. I'd always equated the word prophet with a grey-haired, bearded old guy like Moses or Elijah from Bible times. I had no idea there could be modern-day prophets.

I'd learned to talk to God when I was a child, and I considered Him my closest friend. My family moved a lot when I was growing up, and I suppose in my loneliness I reached out to Him for comfort. I learned to lean on Him, and that helped me as I became an adult and navigated all of life's ups and downs: marriage, raising kids and financial challenges. This time was no exception.

For the past few years, our lives had been filled with financial uncertainty as both Chris and I tried to reinvent ourselves. We'd both started new real estate careers and had built a motel in Pinedale, Wyoming, to cater to the natural gas boom. Chris was making an excellent income as GM of a car dealership.

When the economy crashed, our hopes crashed with it.

The real estate market was stagnant, gas production lagged and the car dealership contracted. Worse yet, we were now badly upside down on our house, along with many other Americans.

Chris took a front line job at another dealership for considerably less income. He tried to run a carpet cleaning business and deal with the motel. I started another career as a loan officer which made very little at the beginning. But that job bought us health insurance. I also did some substitute teaching. Anything we could do to put food on the table.

Times were tough. We had gone from living in our dream home with a lucrative income to wondering how we were going to buy groceries. Several times we were late on our utility bill. I cringed when the doorbell rang, hoping it wasn't the utility worker notifying us that the power was going to be turned off. We used to joke that we were good at robbing Peter to pay Paul, or as Chris put it, "Beating the crap out of Peter in order to pay Paul."

I loved Chris being home more often. The kids and I could spend more time with him. But I could see he was deeply dissatisfied with how things had turned out.

He had always been an amazing provider. In fact, I didn't work a job until our youngest was nearly 4. So I had a good 12-plus years raising my babies and enjoying being a stay-at-home mom.

I had a name for his frustration. I called it his desert time. I was alarmed when he asked me, more than once, "Why am I even here?" It was eye-opening to see the human side of my always-positive husband and understand a bit of the financial pressure he must be feeling.

I spent a lot of time praying for him during these testing times. Just a couple of days before the unplanned church service, he'd said he felt a longing on the inside, a feeling of a void deep within. *What was his purpose?* He wondered. *Was this all there was?* He found himself wanting to be somebody, to make a difference, to leave a legacy for his children and his children's children: a legacy of love, purpose, integrity, character, generosity and eternal values. He knew money comes and money goes, and owning millions of dollars in real estate doesn't fill the void. He was spending a lot of time thinking about where he had been, where he was now and where he was going.

I didn't know it, but a couple of weeks before this church event, Chris had said a prayer asking God to show him why he was here and what his purpose was. He needed to have a purpose, something bigger than simply waking up, working and doing the day-to-day grind. It just wasn't enough anymore. He asked God to give him a legacy.

I couldn't necessarily relate because I was living my dream life. I was married to my best friend and had four beautiful children. I couldn't ask for anything more, other than to see my husband happy and fulfilled. The saying goes, "When mama ain't happy, nobody's happy." Well, this goes both ways, and when daddy isn't happy, then the family just doesn't work anymore.

So yes, while we sat there listening to Tracy the prophet, Chris was definitely ready for a message from God.

The prophet started in again, looking directly at me.

"I keep looking at you, in the pink sweater. Is that your husband next to you? He has his arm around you so I'm assuming he's your husband." The audience laughed.

And then that prophet, his eyes piercing yet kind, looked directly at Chris and began to speak to him.

"Sir, I keep seeing this vacation home… Yes, there it is! I don't see the whole picture, but there is treasure in it. There are generational blessings. I don't see the whole picture but whatever it is, if you can hold onto it, I see treasure chests all around it. God has placed favor on your life. Keep trusting God. Push past every obstacle. Keep memories alive. They are your most valuable asset. The Lord doesn't want you to let go of memories for the sake of anything else. I still see this house. I don't know if you own it, if you are going to buy it, or if it's in the family. Maybe it's a vacation property? Focus on building memories and keeping them alive. There are generational blessings coming down from previous generations and generational blessings you will pass on. Don't relinquish anything. Memories are the most important thing in this season of your life. There will be a flood of life coming to your family, sir."

Beside me, Chris sat rooted to his seat. Our family hung on every word as the prophet continued to speak.

"God is going to re-activate the creative in you. You have an inventive heart. The enemy has tried to lock it up by trials and struggles. In fact he has told you that your best days are behind you, but *your best days are still ahead of you*. He's going to unlock this by rejoicing in the memories. Keep them alive. The creative inventive work is still ahead of you. He's literally going to change your family. *Be resilient.* Don't give up easily. The enemy has tried to break your will. *Don't break.* You're bold enough, you're strong enough and God's hand is upon you. Look at me, man of God. You're a man of God."

By now, tears were running down Chris's face.

"Don't break, you've got it. God's hand is on you for the work of the kingdom. Entrepreneurship is for you. You say, 'But I've struggled here and I've failed here,' but that's the thing with entrepreneurs. Remember when Abraham kept pushing forward? Generational blessings are on your life. Feeding nations, building churches, building God's kingdom... all of that is in your heart. The enemy doesn't like the fact that you're going to do the work of the kingdom. Don't take it personally. The enemy is fighting your calling, not you personally. Something is about to be amazing in your family."

Then he asked to pray for Chris. In his prayer, he mentioned the word memories over and over again.

"The joy of the Lord is your strength, it's your strength. I call in multiple millions and increase and favor. I break off every strategy that has tried to wear you down."

When the prophet had finished, we looked at each other, amazed and perplexed. *What did it all mean?*

Looking back now, it meant the world. For Chris, it made him feel like God saw him and cared about him. For me, it felt like my prayers were heard. Strangely enough, Joya saw it in an entirely different light. She told me that after hearing the prophecy she had a bad feeling that something terrible was about to happen. *How perceptive she was!* All while the rest of us thought it was great and positive and we were celebrating.

How amazing is it to think that God cares about each one of us? Many people don't really know what it feels like to have true love and acceptance. With broken families and tragedies on every hand, we feel insecure. And unfortunately, many young men and women grow up without that acceptance from their earthly fathers.

Chris never had that acceptance. Chris always told me that he felt like God was his father, the One Chris looked up to, knowing he was always watching. His real dad had left home when Chris was two years old, never to be seen again. Then his mom was killed in an airplane crash when he was just 17.

"Believing in God as my Father kept me on the right path," he once told me.

The prophecy captivated our family. We talked about it daily, dreamed about it when we went to sleep at night. We were so excited about what the Lord was going to do in our lives. We told all our close friends and family members about the amazing thing that had happened to us. We shared the church website with anyone who would listen to the prophecy for themselves. Everyone who really knew us could see that this was something special, a message directly to us from God.

And all too soon, those prophetic words would prove much deeper and more meaningful indeed. Because life as we knew it was about to change forever. Just 10 days after we received the prophecy, Chris received a chilling diagnosis that rocked our world.

His best days were ahead. O, how we clung to those words as our neat and tidy existence collapsed around us. That message of hope resonated over and over again. It is still with us to this day. At times those words would be the only thing keeping my husband, children and myself from buckling under our tremendous fear.

The prophet had included me in his prayer, too, saying, "He is releasing strength to you, woman of God."

I didn't realize then how important this simple prayer would be.

THE DIAGNOSIS

Wow, I thought to myself, this is the worst flu bug we've ever seen.

Chris had been in bed for days and complained during the night that his hips were achy. He had a constant headache and some chills. It got so bad that, on the fifth day, I came home early from work with several cans of Lysol and I sprayed Chris's room and even his bed and all around him. I was determined to kill every contagious bug in our house. I sprayed so much that Chris told me he felt like a cockroach.

This is one stubborn flu bug! I don't want the rest of us to get whatever he has.

After I sprayed our house from one end to the other, Jared told me his dad had been hiding a bloody nose from me for a couple of days. Yes, he still had a bloody nose, and yes, he was throwing up blood. Now I was concerned.

Chris asked me to take him to urgent care, which was unheard of. He would rather do just about anything than go to the doctor. I felt calm as I drove him to the urgent care. After all, my healthy, strong Marine husband was just fighting a virus. I was sure a round of antibiotics would do the trick.

Yet as we sat in the waiting room, some doubt crept into my mind. Chris looked incredibly sick. He couldn't stop throwing up, even while in the waiting room. And his bloody nose would not stop bleeding. He waited miserably for the doctor to call him back to the exam room. I felt helpless and impatient. It hurt me to watch him suffer.

After what seemed like an eternity, they took him back to a room. They did the usual things such as taking his temperature. They wanted to do a flu swab, but Chris refused this test. I could see why. They had a foot-long Q-tip that they wanted to shove deeply up his nose, in-between bouts of throwing up. He was in no condition to let them do this. The doctor decided to perform a urine sample, a rather unusual test at this stage. He also performed a blood test, something rarely ordered in urgent care.

As we waited for the results of the blood test, I could tell that Chris was getting worried. He had mentioned during one of his long nights that he hoped he hadn't gotten leukemia or something. It was so random that I brushed these words off easily. *We didn't even have anyone in our immediate families who'd had cancer. Why would he say that?*

When the doctor came back into the room, you could tell he knew something he did not want to say out loud. He told us that Chris's white blood cell count was elevated off the chart to 110,000. He said a normal count was 6,000-10,000.

"Either my machine is broken or Chris is in big trouble," he said.

"How often does your machine break?" I asked.

He said, "Never."

He mentioned the word leukemia. There it was again. In an instant, everything I knew to be true felt like a lie. I felt betrayed, crushed, helpless and overwhelmed.

At the same time, I also felt a surge of something inside me that I knew would make me strong. Stronger than I ever thought I could be.

The only thing I knew about leukemia was that it was the subject of many Hallmark-type movies and the person always died. They were also usually children. *How could my husband have a childhood disease? They must be wrong; the machine really must be broken.* That's what I kept telling myself.

The doctor sent us over to the emergency room of our local hospital, where our long night continued to get stranger. One convenience of being seriously ill is that they do not make you wait in waiting rooms. They took my husband right back and started in on the same routine tests: blood pressure, temperature, urine sample and blood test. As we waited in our room for what seemed like hours, my thoughts were on our children who were all at home, doing homework and having a normal night. We were about to turn their young worlds upside down.

My mind was spinning and I had to get a quick grip on my unruly thoughts.

How are we going to do this? Whatever this is?

How am I going to work?

How are we going to have a normal life and fight this disease at the same time?

How are we going to save my husband?

What am I going to tell my kids, our family?

The doctor came in.

"We believe Chris might have the less serious kind of leukemia," he said. "For now, try not to worry. We're running some more tests."

That made me so happy!

"Don't worry, honey," I told my husband. "You have the good kind! You will probably only have to pop some pills, change your diet, get more sleep, things like that. We can do this."

They wanted us to go home and then head to the cancer center in the morning.

"Be extremely careful," they said. "Your platelets which help with blood clotting are so low that your brain could have a bleed while you sleep or if you bump your head."

Are you crazy? I thought. *You can't just send someone home and tell them not to bleed out, but just to get some sleep and we will deal with things in the morning.*

I called my parents, my brother and Chris's oldest brother and asked them all to pray. Chris and I decided not to worry the kids

21

until we had a definitive diagnosis. So went home, very carefully, and told the kids he would be fine.

I've never felt as scared as I did that night. *Is this the last night I will ever get to sleep with my husband?* My stomach was in complete knots. I did what I knew to do. I started praying. I pushed through the feeling of the black hole in my stomach and begged God to heal my husband and to be with us and to help us sleep. My mind was spinning out of control.

After my prayer, I fell into a deep sleep. I slept soundly and dreamed. During my dream I could hear those comforting words, exactly the way they were spoken to us on the day of the prophecy. It was as if the prophet was in my head and was repeating it word for word while I slept. During my dream, I saw myself standing in the desert, our eldest son Josh by my side. A mighty, rushing wind did a figure eight motion around us, like something out of *Indiana Jones and the Temple of Doom.* In my dream, I knew this wind represented the Holy Spirit.

When I awoke, I pondered the meaning of the dream. *Why did it include our son, and not my husband?* I would soon find out that it was Josh and I who had to be the strongest for the others. I believe the Holy Spirit carried and strengthened us both from that day forward. Josh became the one person I could let my guard down around. Somehow I knew he could handle it. And I could be that place of strength and safety for him, too.

The kids got themselves ready for school so I could call the cancer center at 8:30 a.m. as instructed. Before I even got the chance, they called me and told me to bring Chris in immediately. Once again, my heart lurched with fear. I put Joya in charge of the two boys to get them off to 7th and 10th grades. Then I loaded Chris and his puke bucket into the car. Off we went to find out whether or not my Marine had the good kind or the bad kind.

Our best friends, Pete and Tammie, met us at the cancer center, which was a gracious surprise. Thank God for them. Having them there meant so much. I don't know if we could have gotten through that morning alone.

Once again we sat in a doctor's office waiting for more blood test results. We kept answering the same questions over and over again, which we would get very used to. They, too, thought he had the good kind of leukemia. (Just to set the record straight, there is no good kind).

After hours of waiting, we finally got the results.

It was the other kind.

"You mean the bad kind?" Chris said.

The doctor told him that he was correct.

My horror returned with a vengeance.

Chris had always told me if he ever got cancer he wouldn't do chemotherapy. He had heard too many stories about suffering from the side effects.

"What if I choose not to do treatment," Chris asked. "What then? How much time would I have?"

"Two weeks if you're lucky," the doctor said matter of factly

Chris looked at me.

"Well," he said, "then let's get 'er done!"

The doctor said a lot more words, which seemed to ramble on and felt like someone was talking from a faraway planet. What I did hear was that we needed to go straight to the hospital in the big city nearby where they could treat us. That doctor would be waiting and we did not even have time to grab an overnight bag. There was no talk of getting a second opinion. They wanted us there immediately to start treatment.

We went out to the waiting room to update our best friends. We'd been through a lot together over the last 15 or so years, but never matters of life and death. The looks on their faces said it all. They looked absolutely shocked and scared. They wished us well as we headed to the hospital, while they made plans to pick up our three kids from school and bring them to the hospital later in the afternoon. They promised not to say anything to them about the diagnosis. I would plan to tell the kids once they got to the hospital.

Chris was so, so miserably sick. That 45-minute drive to the hospital was agonizingly long. He kept throwing up bright red blood and he looked like death warmed over. We got to the hospital and since it was our first time there, we were confused as to where to park and what to do. So we parked blocks away and proceeded to walk uphill to the hospital entrance. I'm still not sure how my husband did this in his weakened state, but we were on autopilot.

We got Chris checked in and the whirlwind began. Even though we were in the fight of our lives, I felt strangely peaceful. My head was spinning, but my heart and soul were strong, calm and even hopeful. I couldn't help but remember those words that we had heard just a few days earlier.

Chris's best days are ahead of him.

I kept reminding him of those words. No matter what I was feeling, I tried my absolute hardest to find something positive for us to focus on. When I talked to my dad, he asked me what we needed.

"I need my mom!" I said.

Just hours later Mom would arrive by air. Our friends were already on the way with our three youngest kids. I found out later my teenagers had driven home from school at breakneck speeds, crying all the way.

One diagnosis, and so many people already affected, so many reactions.

Now I would have to give my kids the news. They were heavy on my mind.

How are they going to be taken care of while I am at the hospital and everything is so uncertain? Yes they're independent, but they still need a mom, a dad. They need normal life routines!

For a helicopter mom, this was going to be a trying time. I would have to let go of worrying and just trust God that they would be okay.

Now nothing mattered but surviving. Not our bills, not what was for dinner, not school supplies, not our pets, our jobs, our business. *Nothing.* Only saving my husband's life. Everything else was insignificant and our priorities were instantly clear.

I called Josh at Boise State University. I also told the rest of my family and Chris's oldest brother. Unfortunately, Chris and his middle brother were out of touch, with many relationship ups and downs over the years.

Once our three youngest kids arrived at the hospital, our friends left the room so that I could look our kids in the eyes and explain what was going on. Somehow I managed to tell them their dad had this disease called acute lymphoblastic leukemia, or ALL. I had to tell them it was very aggressive and that he had to start treatment immediately, but that there was a treatment plan in place and we hoped for the best possible outcome. I tried to keep a positive spin on some pretty grim news so that they wouldn't freak out. But I also tried very hard throughout our ordeal to keep it real. I never wanted to lie to my kids about their dad's condition. I still remember the looks on their faces, their tears, their questions.

I remember Chris's oncologist coming into the room and drawing a bunch of little circles, representing cells, on a white board to try to explain what was going on in Chris's body. Although I got quickly lost somewhere between his Croatian accent and the science of T-cells, I would soon come to be an expert in leukemia, and not by choice.

From the first impression we loved Chris's doctor. He was a bundle of energy. He told you like it was. No sugar coating anything and that's the way Chris liked it. We had lots of questions for the doctor. *What were Chris's actual chances of beating this?* Other questions came to me from the kids, my parents, our friends, Chris's brother. Apparently this was a childhood leukemia, very treatable in children. But in grownups? Not so treatable. We heard all kinds of facts on survival odds and treatment details. When it came to the bone marrow transplant part of the treatment, the doctor told Chris he was "too young and good looking" to have a say in the matter. He was going to go forward with the treatment, no matter what. I think the doctor knew if Chris was going to have any shot at a future the bone marrow transplant was non-negotiable. However, we did have the option to say no and Chris seriously thought about not doing it.

There would be a 10 percent chance of survival with the chemotherapy only, and a 50 percent chance of survival with the bone marrow transplant. That was if everything went perfectly, and of course at this stage there was no mention of any long-lasting side effects.

Surviving... that was the only thing on all of our minds.

This wouldn't be easy. In fact, it would be the hardest thing Chris had ever gone through, said doctor. He would have up to 14 hospital stays of one week each minimum during the chemotherapy. This is where I started to lose track. Something about more chemotherapy, total body radiation, a bone marrow transplant, living in Seattle for four months.. what?

Even after all that, he was given a 50 percent chance of so-called long term survival, or more than five years. Without any treatment, death was absolutely certain.

I could barely comprehend what the doctor was telling us.

All I know is that I want my best friend to live. To see his daughter graduate, walk her down the aisle, to see our boys grow up and turn into men. Chris always dreamed of having grandchildren and of taking me to Italy. But right now, in this moment, all I want for him is to wake up tomorrow. And the next day, and the next.

All I could do was tend to Chris, offer him moral support and try my best to comfort him. The nurses were already ordering all kinds of tests and procedures that had to be done before the chemo started.

The picc line was a thin piece of plastic tubing that had to be inserted in his upper arm each and every time Chris got chemo in the hospital. That procedure itself was a big ordeal for someone who hated needles and hospitals. The tubing wound around and settled into his heart. This way the medicine could be delivered to his body easier with less risk of infection. I could tell it scared him to have the picc line go into his arm. One time the technician ran the picc line the wrong way and it was blowing bubbles behind Chris's eyes. She said, "Oops, that's not where we want it!"

There were also bone marrow tests, which were extremely

painful. There were liver tests, heart tests and brain tests. There were lumbar punctures, to see if the leukemia was in Chris's spinal fluid. Also painful. This kind of leukemia is known for moving into the brain (or testicles in men) so they wanted to make sure it wasn't there already. The bone marrow test helped determine what kind of chromosomes were involved. These chromosomes make a difference in people's prognosis. So all in all, he had acute lymphoblastic leukemia with T cell 8 deformity. Not good news, by any means, but not the worst possible news.

There is a silver lining! Nothing in his spinal fluid. So the goal is to hit this cancer hard, get into a good remission, keep it in remission for six months or so while receiving the other treatments and looking for a possible donor, until his body is ready to receive the bone marrow transplant.

Throughout, I'd called our son Josh frequently to update him on what was going on. I could hear his concern through the phone. And before I knew it, there was Josh, standing at the doorway of the hospital room. He had dropped out of college, driven the eight hours home on icy roads, and was ready to play his part to help. As bad as I felt that he had dropped out of college, it was the best feeling in the entire world to see him standing there. Right then, he stepped up to the plate and became the man of the family while his dad was tethered to a hospital bed by plastic tubing, with some kind of poison that had to have skull and crossbones on the container pumping through his veins.

The chemotherapy was so dangerous that the kids and I weren't even allowed to use Chris's bathroom. We could have some bad side effects from that. These were the same drugs that were flowing through my husband's veins day in and day out. The nurses who administered this chemo had to gown up and wear special gloves and plastic face shields to protect themselves, but I was supposed to trust this was good for my husband?

People tell you to get a second opinion, but in this case we didn't have time for that. Another 24 hours at home and Chris may have had an aneurysm in his brain. His platelets were incredibly low and getting lower every day. There was no time to talk to more doctors, search the internet for options or maybe try a more naturopathic approach.

We were facing life and death and we had no time to ponder options.

OUR NEW NORMAL

"THE WAY I SEE IT, IF YOU WANT THE RAINBOW YOU GOTTA PUT
UP WITH THE RAIN." —DOLLY PARTON

T hat first week, I stayed with Chris every day and night. There was very little sleep since the nurses came in on the hour. My mom stayed with the kids while they continued to go to school. I hoped this would help keep them busy and distract them from the reality we now faced as a family.

I'm really glad I stayed that first week. His nurses couldn't be everywhere at once, so he needed my help going to the bathroom, eating and throwing up. The first few chemo treatments made him extremely weak and dizzy. I was always worried he might keel over and hit the floor when the nurses weren't watching, which did in fact happen one time on my watch.

Once Chris got used to the hospital routine and began to feel better from the initial chemo treatments, I was able to stay with him during the day and go home at night to be with the kids. I'd never realized all the things my husband took care of, including the house, the yard, my car, our business, our finances or even his role in disciplining and encouraging the kids. I tried my best to help them with homework, do laundry and simply be a mom.

But Chris soon had a new and scary complication. There were so many dead cancer cells in his blood that his kidneys almost shut down. I couldn't imagine going through this multiple times. I would whisper to myself those comforting words from Matthew 6:34, a verse I had known since I was a child.

Refuse to worry about tomorrow but deal with each challenge that comes your way. One day at a time, tomorrow will take care of itself.

Now more than ever I needed this reminder. Every day I visited Chris, worked remotely at my loan officer job and did all my regular household and mommy duties when I got home. I also began the daunting task of updating everyone in our circle every time there was a medical update, prayer request or other news. That alone became a full-time job.

Everything was a whirlwind. I will always thank God for friends and family who stepped in to help in these trying times. In a desperate hour like this, you really do find out who your friends are. Those who were there for us will never be forgotten. I remember thinking, *Nothing I do will ever repay them, short of maybe donating them an organ.*

It felt strange accepting help from others. Chris and I always liked to be on the giving end of things, not the receiving. But by the time help started pouring in, I knew we were in over our heads. That humbled us fast. I understood God wanted us to receive with open arms any good thing that people did for us or gave us.

Don't relinquish anything, the prophecy said.

I realized the gifts gave their givers purpose and joy. I think they were also expressing gratitude for their own good health. People really are amazing. Friends and acquaintances we hadn't spoken to in decades called us, sent gift cards for the kids and put checks in the mail. So many people sent their prayers. Our friends brought many dinners over for the kids. On those many nights when I stayed late at the hospital, it brought me great peace to know that my kids had dinner. And my friends must know me too well, because I lost count of how many Starbucks cards I received.

You never know how much a small act of kindness means. Believe me, each act made all the difference. Some days it was the only thing that kept us going.

During that time, Chris was in and out of the hospital for treatments. Driving him there was a 45-minute ordeal every time. We'd have to stop at least a couple of times for him to throw up on the side of the road.

Every time, he needed to stay for a week or longer. I would drop the kids off for school, maybe stop by my office if I had something pressing that I couldn't do from the hospital, then head to the hospital with my laptop in hand. There, I would walk the halls with Chris and watch him sleep, or throw up or whatever else he was dealing with in that moment. Meanwhile, I'd continue to take phone calls from real estate agents and customers, always doing my best to sound like nothing was wrong. Most of them had no idea that Chris was throwing up in the background thanks to that handy *Mute* button on my phone. Despite my best efforts, I actually had a couple of clients who found out what we were dealing with and decided to go somewhere else for their loan.

"We don't want to bother you," they said.

Please bother me, I thought. *I need a distraction from watching my sick husband sleep. And I need the income now more than ever.*

I would bring him clean pajamas to change into, help him shower, change his bedsheets, read to him and generally keep him company. To help comfort him, I would play our recorded prophecy over and over. And I would play the worship music he loved now more than ever, songs like *I Can Only Imagine, Good to be Alive* and many others. Sometimes I would just lay with him while he slept or rested. Once he was settled I would work. There were days I couldn't get much work done at all and had to catch it up when I got home at night.

Chris did a lot of sleeping. The chemo just wiped him out. Or I would sit and listen to him talk about his concerns, his life and his fears. Sometimes I simply watched the tears run down my tough Marine's cheeks.

"I wonder if I'll live to see my grandbabies," he would choke out. "Or if I'll even be able to see Joya graduate?"

He wanted so badly to live. But he had to face the reality that this might not work. He might not find a donor or the leukemia might come back. For the first time in our lives, we felt completely out of control. Of course, control is always just an illusion, but facing this fearsome giant made it all too clear.

We found ourselves with conflicting emotions. We willed so desperately that Chris might live, while we tried wholeheartedly to trust in God's plan for his life, whatever that might be.

It's strange to watch the person you love most grappling with his own life's fragility. We know death is always a possibility and it could all be over in an instant. We are all just one heartbeat away. We could drop dead, get hit by a car or even choke on a bite of food. But coming face-to-face with the actual prospect of death? That is something else entirely.

I will tell you that when staring into the great unknown together, nothing is left unsaid. We had many tender moments, Chris and I. As awful as it was, it was also precious time together. After late nights in that hospital room, I now know what is real and truly in my husband's heart. For that I will be forever grateful.

Some nights I struggled with the prospect of becoming a widow at 42. I knew that a single plot twist, something as simple as the common cold, could mean certain death.

Yet I also knew there was hope. Hope certainly in statistics and in science, but incredible hope from on high.

Your best days are ahead of you.

Since these are not his best days, they must be in the future.

After I stayed as long as I could, I would leave the hospital. I could tell Chris didn't want me to go. It tugged at my heart every time I left him in the care of the nurses, God and the angels, as I drove back home to my children, my home, my dog, my job and my regular life. I usually called my mom on the drive home to update her on his status. Even though she was far away, she was a huge support and I felt her presence close to me. *Thank you, Mom.*

I was absolutely drained at the end of each day. I was getting up early, doing the household things moms do, then putting in a full day's work somehow between the drive to and from the hospital and while I was there. At home I'd finish work, do the evening chores, help the kids with homework and try to answer their questions about their dad. Often one or more of the kids would be crying when I got home. I would do my best to comfort and console them, but also make sure I was being completely honest with them. I will never forget the night when my 11-year-old crumpled into my lap and told me he didn't want his daddy to die. I cried along with him.

"I don't want daddy to die either," I said through my own sobs. " But we have to remember that, live or die, God has your daddy in His hands."

I also reminded my kids about the prophecy.

"Remember what the prophet said, that your father's best days are ahead of him? Last I checked, he still hasn't invented anything, fed any nations or built any churches yet. God still has plenty of work for him to do."

And we would pray together. Then I would then drop into bed, pray for my husband and family, then do it all over again the next day. I really missed sleeping with my husband. There are so many things that we take for granted. In the night, my thoughts raced.

Would this be my new way of life? Alone in my bed? Husbandless?

But as soon as my mind started to wander, I would remember to pray. I begged and pleaded with God to spare Chris. I thanked Him for the beautiful times we had together and I prayed for forgiveness for the times I treated him less than the gift that he was. Philippians 4:6-7 was a powerful reminder in my darkest hours of doubt.

Don't be pulled in different directions or worried about a thing. Be saturated in prayer throughout each day, offering your faith-filled requests before God with overflowing gratitude. Tell him every detail of your life, then God's wonderful peace that transcends human understanding will make the answers known to you through Jesus Christ.

The kids soldiered through life and continued to excel, despite the uncertainty looming over our family. They amazed me. They still gave it their all on the basketball court, football field and baseball field, at their jobs and school events.

Their dad watched them play from the stands whenever he could get out of the hospital. He was easy to spot, because, long before COVID-19, he was the only person wearing a medical mask. He might have thrown up in the parking lot to get there, but he was there nonetheless.

At times it was just me at the events because Chris was either in the hospital or too sick to go out. Other times I would have to be at the hospital, too, and the kids would just have to grab a lift with a teammate.

Through it all, Chris remained positive.

"How are you doing?" people would ask.

"Perfect," he would say.

That was and is always still his answer. I have seen my husband in the worst possible physical condition and his answer remains the same. *Perfect.*

As the doctors made their rounds, they'd ask Chris how he was doing.

"Perfect," he always said. "And how are you doing?"

He would accept nothing less than an enthusiastic answer in response.

"Life is amazing," he would say. "So amazing we can't waste a single second of it not being perfect."

My husband was the cheerleader of his entire 7th floor.

For me, coming home to three teenagers and one young adult was actually a mental reprieve. I could get lost in their youthful dramas for a few hours. I had to trust that God had Chris in His hands and that the nurses were taking care of him so I could be present for my kids. God would remind me that this was Chris's battle and I couldn't fight it for him. Then the week would be over and we'd get to bring Chris home again.

I get to sleep with my husband again! I get to wake up next to him! Only now he smells like a plastic factory and chemicals. Now I need to keep the kids quiet while daddy rested.

Our home was always a place where our kids' friends wanted to be. It was like they were an extra part of our family. And it was no different with Chris home.

The friends would come in the front door, glance over to our bedroom, see Chris in the bed and say hello to him. Or sometimes they would all end up sitting around him, having heart-to-heart talks about jobs, cars, life or girls. They would also see firsthand the side effects of cancer and chemotherapy.

One time our middle son Jordan had two of his buddies over. Chris had just eaten a bowl of fruit loops. His body promptly threw them back up intact into his bowl. It had happened so fast he didn't have time to run to the garbage can. The boys were wide-eyed.

"Those fruit loops were still cold on the way back up," he said. "I could probably just eat them again"

Black humor is normal in the world of cancer, and so is throwing up. It's like breathing, it happens so often, despite all the medications to stifle it.

But that's the way Chris was. Even in the midst of it all, he tried to make other people comfortable. His first thought always ran to others, not to himself. Even from his hospital bed he would be thinking of me.

"Do you need anything?" he would ask. "Can I get you something to drink? Do you need me to rub your feet?

Who is this man I married? Who thinks like that?

His character amazed me. Because of cancer, I got to appreciate a side of Chris that had always been there but I had been too blind or busy to see.

January came and went. Then February. Basketball ended and baseball began, along with school dances, driver's licenses and first dates. Work continued to be busy. Somehow I was able to keep all the balls in the air. There were times I felt like I could lose my mind, but then I would remember who held the world together.

Cancer sliced through our lives like a razor-sharp knife. Life became very simple. We knew exactly what was important and what wasn't. In those ways, it was a blessed time for our family. I found most things that used to be important were no longer important at all. I found myself noticing the good in life, the sparkle in the dew of morning. I found it forced me to appreciate the simplest of victories, to count every blessing and find every silver lining.

We'd heard the wise saying:

Cancer can make you bitter or make you better.

As a family, we decided better was the only way.

THE ANOINTING

"PRAY FOR ONE ANOTHER SO THAT YOU MAY BE HEALED." —
JAMES 5:16

B oy, does bad news travel fast.

Dwain and Misty Fish, our friends from Jackson Hole, heard of Chris's diagnosis and got ahold of our son Josh.

"Josh, how do you feel about the situation?" Dwain asked.

"I feel hopeful," Josh told him. "Our family received a prophecy at church, and I have complete faith that my dad is going to be okay."

His faith was strong enough to spur Dwain to action. A former pastor, he loaded up his family and drove straight through the night, for 13 hours on icy roads, to come and physically pray for Chris.

"I feel very strongly that God wants us to put our faith into action," he said. "I don't want to be one of those Christians who say, 'We will pray for you,' and then go on about their lives."

For us, this was Christ in action. We will forever be grateful for his obedience.

Misty told him that it might be imposing on us for them to drop by unannounced, so before they showed up, she made sure he texted me to see if it was okay. I didn't hesitate. This diagnosis had stripped me of my pride. I didn't care anymore if my hair didn't look quite right that morning, or even whether or not I'd showered. I didn't care how I came across to a friend.

Maybe in the past I would have been too proud to let them come. I wouldn't have wanted to ask for help. But now, I no longer cared that my husband might not want to be seen in a hospital gown or appear sick, or helpless or even scared. All I cared about was his healing. I knew my husband was facing the challenge of a lifetime, and I wasn't about to let pride get in the way of his healing.

Dwain read to us from James 5:14-16.

"Is anyone among you sick? Then he must call for the elders of the church and they are to pray over him, anointing him with oil in the name of the Lord; and the prayer offered in faith will restore the one who is sick, and the Lord will raise him up, and if he has committed sins, they will be forgiven him. Therefore, confess your sins to one another, and pray for one another so that you may be healed. The effective prayer of a righteous man can accomplish much."

Yes, Lord, I believed then, and still believe today in the power of prayer.

Chris had asked me to send them a copy of our prophecy that they could listen to as they drove.

"They should know what God has projected for our future before they feel sorry for us or doubt His power," he said.

And God responded. On the way, God impressed Dwain to purchase a brand-new container of grape juice and olive oil so we could have communion in the hospital. He told Dwain He would provide the people to anoint Chris with oil, and that Dwain was to lead the prayer only.

It just so happened that some of our best friends were with us, two couples, Pete and Tammie and Doug and Sheila, when Dwain and Misty arrived. Dwain directed the two men to each rub the olive oil on Chris's feet, while we all prayed for his healing. Looking back now, we giggle about the fact that two grown men, men's men, manly men, were rubbing Chris's feet there in that hospital room. It was one of the most beautiful moments I have ever witnessed, as if we were participants in a modern-day Bible story.

We had communion together and thanked our Lord for dying on the cross for us and giving his body for healing our diseases. We read 1 Peter 2:24.

"And He Himself bore our sins in His body on the cross, so that we might die to sin and live to righteousness; for by His wounds you were healed".

This was not the everyday norm for our family, so it took a lot of faith to believe in this divine moment. We went to church occasionally, and we knew God was able to do anything, but to apply it to an actual life-and-death situation in our own family went much deeper. We didn't care what the nurses thought of our anointing. All we wanted was to pray for the man lying there in that hospital bed: The friend, the husband, the lover, the father. We prayed for nearly four hours, yet it felt like mere minutes. When we were done, Chris was actually glowing. Was it the blessing or the chemo?

Our friends departed for the evening to get some much-needed rest and the pastor and his wife came to visit from the church where we had received the prophecy. We didn't know these people. We had attended another church in town for the past decade, but the people standing in front of us were new to us. I still can't get over the fact that they cared enough to come visit and pray for Chris.

Raydeane, the pastor's wife, had survived cancer three times. She brought Chris a book written by a fellow cancer warrior, called *To See Another Sunrise* by Jim Morrison. When Pastor J.O. prayed, he quoted James 5:14-15.

Coincidence? Not to me.

I would continue to hear that verse over and over in the near future. It was clear to me that God wanted us to focus on this scripture.

They asked how Chris was doing.

"This is actually the best day of my life," he said.

"Wait a minute," I said. "I don't understand. Here you are, hooked up to monitors while being poked and prodded and tested, and this is the best day of your life? What on earth do you mean?"

"I had a vision," he said. "I was looking back over my life. I saw that I had hold of God's hand but I was trying to lead God instead of the other way around. It's like I was saying, It's okay, God, you can come along with me and *be a part of* my life.' But this time, God is doing the leading and I need to learn how to surrender and give up control."

This vision gave Chris great peace. After that, he knew God was either going to heal him or he would end up with Jesus in Heaven. This was a win-win. He also had a complete new appreciation for life in general. He would never take another sunrise for granted and to him, the eternal optimist, this was a special gift.

HE MADE US GO BACK TO CHURCH

"YOUR TESTIMONY IS THE STORY OF YOUR ENCOUNTER WITH
GOD AND WHAT ROLE HE HAS PLAYED THROUGHOUT YOUR
LIFE."

That next day was Sunday and our friends from Wyoming were still in town. I wanted us all to go to the hospital and spend the day with Chris. But Chris said no.

His only wish that day was for me to take our friends, my mom and the kids to church. I tried talking him out of it but he insisted. So we honored his request.

It was an amazing service. Pastor J.O. mentioned Chris during his sermon. He told the congregation how Chris had received a prophecy and then gotten sick, how Pastor J.O. and Raydeane had seen him the previous day, how Chris had said it was the best day of his life. The entire church prayed for him and our family. We all sat crying in the chairs. It was a very touching moment and hard to describe.

A young boy from the congregation asked the pastor if he could read something he felt God had given him for Chris.

No way. James 5:14-15. I couldn't get away from that Bible passage if I tried.

Believe me, James is etched in my mind forever. If I ever hear of someone who is sick, that chapter is the first thing I think of.

The prayer of faith. I also love verses 16, 17 and 18.

"Confess your sins to each other and pray for each other so that you may be healed. The earnest prayer of a righteous person has great power and produces wonderful results. Elijah was as human as we are, and yet when he prayed earnestly that no rain would fall none fell for three and a half years. Then, when he prayed again, the sky sent down rain and the earth began to yield its crops."

Prayer works. No, we don't get everything we pray for. And we don't always understand why. God's ways are not our ways and his thoughts are not our thoughts. So why not take the chance and pray? I'm so very glad we did. We're just regular people. Our family has fights and we cuss. We are far from perfect. So it amazes me that the God of the Universe hears our prayers.

I have seen firsthand that our prayers, our faith and our attitude are everything. We cannot choose what life throws at us, but we can choose how we will react.

I would not have reacted like Chris did. I complain more when I catch a cold than my husband has in the years since he was diagnosed. I do believe God truly knows what we each can handle. As 1 Corinthians 10:13 says, "We all experience times of testing, which is normal for every human being. But God will be faithful to you. He will screen and filter the severity, nature and timing of every test or trial that you face so that you can bear it. And each test is an opportunity to trust him more, for along with every trial God has provided for you a way of escape that will bring you out of it victoriously."

God knew Chris could handle this challenge the same way he has handled many others; head on, with an amazing attitude, looking for the good.

Our friends and my mom had to return home. Gratefully, the gift cards, meals and support kept coming. I did my very best to succeed at my job, raise a family and offer moral support to my warrior of a husband, who was now in the biggest battle of his life.

IT'S NOT ABOUT YOU!

"ONLY GOD CAN TURN A MESS INTO A MESSAGE, A TEST INTO A TESTIMONY, A TRIAL INTO A TRIUMPH AND A VICTIM INTO A VICTORY."

It was hard to recognize Chris without his hospital gown.

He was back home from another long stay at his oncology hospital, a place I'd taken to calling Hotel Sacred Heart. It had felt liberating but scary when I wheeled him out those doors and into the fresh winter air.

With him in his favorite chair back home, it almost felt like we were back in our old lives again, before the ugly cancer monster reared its head.

That next morning I was sitting propped up in my bed and having a conversation with God. Really, it was more of a one-sided pity party than a conversation.

I keep thinking about our prophecy, I told God. *I can't shake those words. God, what was that about? I asked you to talk to Chris and you gave us a message about memories? Being resilient? A house? I have no idea what any of it means! Are we any better off than we were before you spoke to us?*

Oh and by the way, I continued, *whoever said I had any interest in feeding nations or building churches?*

Yes, I actually said those words to God. And that's when God replied.

It's not about YOU.

I clearly heard those words in my heart or head or wherever

you hear from God besides a burning bush. By His tone I recognized that I needed to get with the program. This wasn't the "still, small voice" I had grown accustomed to hearing inside of my heart. This voice was something else.

I knew I had no business questioning God. But as a human, God understands why we question him and act bratty sometimes. Psalm 103:14 says, "For He knows our mortal frame; He remembers that we are merely dust."

It's a wonder God puts up with me, or any of us for that matter. I can be a little rebel. Thankfully, the greatness of His love and his mercy is impossible to understand.

"But Christ proved God's passionate love for us by dying in our place *while we were lost and ungodly*" —Romans 5:8.

This certainly wasn't the last time I heard from God during our cancer journey. But it was a turning point.

That day, propped up in my bed, I stopped questioning God and started thanking him for his perfect plan. I realized God uses humans for his plans and purposes and sometimes it isn't what we would have planned for ourselves. It might be a little or a lot uncomfortable. He uses absolutely everything, and doesn't waste a single opportunity to turn it for our good. As a believer in Jesus my life really isn't about me. It's about reaching The One. It's trusting God's plan for me and trusting that it's a good plan. As Luke 15:4-5 says, "There once was a shepherd with a hundred lambs, but one of his lambs wandered away and was lost. So the shepherd left the ninety-nine lambs out in the open field and searched in the wilderness for that one lost lamb. He didn't stop until he finally found it. With exuberant joy he raised it up and placed it on his shoulders, carrying it back with cheerful delight."

So this cancer journey we were on had to be another one of God's genius plans. I must have faith that He was in the process of using my husband for the highest good. I didn't want to be left behind.

From that day forward, I moved in faith, trusting Him with all that I had regardless of the outcome. This is what my husband has always told me true faith is.

"Now faith brings our hopes into reality and becomes the foundation needed to acquire the things we long for. It is all the evidence required to prove what is still unseen." Hebrews 11:1.

It's like the story of Abraham, childless and very old, being told by God that he would have many descendants. God took him outside and told him to look up at the stars. He told him that his descendants would look like a sky full of stars. Did he know for sure this would happen? How could he? Yet God gave him something tangible to look at: the stars in the sky.

I also believe the tangible thing he gave our family was the prophecy, telling us "Your best days are ahead of you." That was our sky full of stars. That is what we focused on and still focus on each and every day.

Abraham saw with his own eyes how old he and Sarah were. And yet he believed in the impossible. If we want big things to happen, we must also believe, especially when all the cards are stacked against us. Is this a guarantee? Only God can answer that. I know one thing. If and when my own ship goes down, I will go down believing and I will go down full of hope.

THE LIFE OF A CANCER PATIENT

"ONE MAN WITH GOD IS A MAJORITY." —BROTHER ANDREW

When a hospital is your home away from home, and you are a people person like Chris, you meet a cast of characters.

Maria, the cleaning lady, was one of his favorites. She would always brighten his day with their conversations and her home-made cookies. What a precious spirit. What a gift each act of kindness can be.

Maria would smile and hand me a necklace or a picture frame.

"We need to keep praying for Chris," she would say. "It don't cost no dinero!"

All the nurses made such a difference. They helped us absorb the bad news and celebrated with us when we got a good report. They pampered Chris and our whole family. They'd get the kids ice cream bars and extra pillows and blankets when we stayed over. They are all saints.

Our doctor was the most amazing person. Even though he dealt with cancer day in and day out, he was always upbeat with an enthusiastic smile. His sense of humor was a blessing. One morning when I called Chris, the doctor was standing beside his bed. The phone lit up with *sexymomma*, which Chris had labeled me in his phone contacts. To this day, the doctor still calls me sexy momma. Another time we were discussing whether or not our kids could be bone marrow transplant donors and I mistakenly asked the doc, "Can our kids be boners?" Chris and I and the doctor all had a good laugh over this one. You have to find things to laugh about or else the ugliness of cancer and its treatment can be overwhelming.

As a family, we've always tried to find the humor in every situation. Why else would *Step Brothers* be our favorite movie? That was a gift Chris gave all of us. He's one of the funniest people ever. And all four of our kids have gotten his sense of humor. My sense of humor is more sarcastic in nature, which can also be very funny at times. Only my daughter and mom ever think I'm funny, even though I crack myself up all the time.

It was a new experience for me to see Chris chained to the chemo pole and in a hospital gown. He was a great patient. For the most part, he did what he was told. He tried his best to lift everyone's mood.

After each stay in the hospital for chemo treatments, Chris was released and allowed to be at home as long as he was careful not to get sick. The chemotherapy killed his good blood cells along with the cancer cells, leaving him with virtually no functioning immune system during the duration of treatments. Still, we tried to live semi-normal lives. We'd go out and about, with Chris wearing a mask, using hand sanitizer and avoiding people. But it's hard to dodge all the germs, especially when you have four kids at home and even some of their friends.

With his compromised immune system, he was not allowed to eat fresh fruit due to risk of listeria, salmonella and E. coli. He was also not allowed to eat at buffets. Prior to his diagnosis, he'd loved to go to the casino for the all-you-can-eat crab buffet, a treat that had become a family tradition. We did cheat a few times and sneak away to the buffet. I chalked it up as a morale booster because he really, really wanted it. Strangely enough, the only things he was hungry for during this time were frozen yogurt and fresh fruit. So that made eating tough.

After a weeklong round of chemo, it took his body another

week to bounce back. So he would spend that week at home recovering, then go back for another hospital stay.

No story about chemo would be complete with Chris and his radioactive pee. That was one of the many strange and harrowing, but also humorous events along our cancer journey. The nurses had given him a pee bottle in case he couldn't get to the bathroom in time. He had used that, but in the middle of the night, his accuracy must understandably have left something to be desired. The next day, he kept saying that the bottoms of his feet were really sore. We chalked it up as another mystery cancer symptom, until we finally realized what the problem was. His feet were corroded from chemo pee. In fact, whatever chemicals had been in that pee were so strong that the linoleum tiles next to his bed were eroding. *Wow!*

In between hospital visits, we tried to get him as much sleep as possible. We went in for lab work and a number of red blood cell and platelet transfusions. I lost count at 37. He was constantly getting his blood drawn to see what type of blood product he would need. We learned that blood and other blood products, along with medications to boost white blood cell production, are a common need during leukemia treatment.

He received a series of injections to increase his white blood cell count, and these made his bones ache.

Those were some of the worst nights, when Chris couldn't sleep from the pain. One night I had difficulty getting pain meds in time, and after that, our doctor gave us his personal cell number and told me to call any time of the day or night if we ever needed anything. I bet he's sorry he told me that! I tried not to bug him unless it was important, but cancer patients have all kinds of problems that arise that need a doctor's attention.

A typical day out of the hospital involved driving from Coeur d'Alene to Spokane for a blood or platelet transfusion. Each transfusion took 3-5 hours. The blood had to be typed and crossed, meaning it was tested for compatibility in the hopes of avoiding any adverse reaction. For some reason, it was always difficult to get a needle into Chris's body. Usually after someone spent five tries digging for a vein, an ER nurse would have to come up and do it.

Many days I felt overwhelmed.

I might just lose my mind today.

But if I fall apart, who is going to be the mom and caregiver?

So I would push that thought away. I told myself I would possibly entertain it on another day. That happened many, many days. And I haven't lost it, not yet. I found the trick was not to entertain the negative thought for more than a split second.

God must have known I would need a flexible career when I became a loan officer. As long as I had my laptop, I could work from my car, the doctor's office or the hospital. It wasn't easy and sometimes it took a lot of creativity, but it was always possible. In the midst of it all, I could feel the Lord's arms wrapped around me. Everyone kept telling me, "You're so strong!" Yet I wasn't. God was carrying me.

Early in our cancer journey, my mother gave me some wonderful advice. And she continued to call me, nearly every single day, and remind me again.

"Honey, make sure you do one thing today just for *YOU*. I don't care if that means you get a latte. Something that simple. But make sure you do."

It was so great when Chris got the new blood because it perked him up and gave him some energy. On the other hand, we could tell when his platelets were getting low because these tiny red spots, called petechiae, would begin to appear all over his body.

On one memorable occasion, we visited a hospital in a new town on the way to watch our son play baseball. Our entire family trouped in together for the transfusion. Once again, the nurse was having a hard time finding a vein. As the needle dug deeper into his arm, I heard a noise behind me, and turned just in time to see Joya faint right there and topple over. Luckily one of her brothers was able to help break her fall. The story ended well, since we finally found a nurse who was able to get a vein. We got Chris his blood transfusion and several hours later we hit the road to complete our trip and watch our son's weekend baseball tournament. The tale of Joya passing out has been a family legend ever since.

Those three and a half months were filled with countless blood transfusions, chemotherapy treatments, one head shaving party, many hospital stays, numerous doctor visits, hundreds of blood tests, x-rays, CT scans, MRIs, bone marrow tests, spinal taps, many pills, lots of vomiting, lots of driving and lots of waiting.

But there was also lots of family time, most of it gathered around Chris's bed, and tons of memories made. Somehow Chris was able to keep our out-of-state motel running with his cell phone, plenty of delegating and the sheer grace of God.

And then our amazing friends decided to have a fundraiser for us. At first we felt so weird about it. We felt like mooches. But early on in our cancer journey I made a deal with God. I promised that we would pay forward any kind thing that was done for us.

And we took the prophecy at its word. We were *not to relinquish anything.* Relinquish means to voluntarily cease to keep or claim; to give up. Other ways to say relinquish would be to give away, hand over, lay down, let go of, yield, surrender or walk away from.

So Chris and I had a serious heart-to-heart about the fundraiser. We realized it would have been a slap in God's face not to cheerfully receive the beautiful provision He was providing for us through people. If we were not good receivers, we realized, we would be robbing the givers of joy.

During our cancer journey, my faith in the human race increased 100-fold. And through that journey, I learned to never turn our backs on anyone who we can possibly help in return. After all, we are all going through a hard time of some kind or another. When someone you love is hurting or sick, and it seems there's nothing you can do to fix them, simply give them a meal or say a prayer. Do the smallest thing that is within your power to do. It may seem insignificant to you, but it will mean the world to the person who is hurting.

The fundraiser was a huge success. The money helped us pay for medical and travel expenses. Even when you have insurance, cancer is still so expensive. We made payments to hospitals for years after treatment. Chris was still looking pretty good and feeling pretty good, so he was able to enjoy the fundraiser.. People we hadn't seen in years showed up, with friends, acquaintances, co-workers and the like all joining together to support our grateful family. People we barely knew came up to me and handed me checks for amounts as large as $1,000. We even had some anonymous donations.

Most importantly, countless people told me they were praying for Chris, a priceless gift indeed.

We learned a lot by sitting in the waiting room of the cancer center for check ups. There the world of cancer is on display for all to see. We met patients in every phase of treatment. We got to see what we could "look forward to."

And sometimes there would be an empty seat, a cancer warrior we had come to love who had fought their last fight.

The people we met inspired us so much with their positive attitudes and faith. And we knew how fortunate we really were. At least we had a treatment plan and the possibility of a good outcome. Some of the people we met were on their fourth clinical trial and there was nothing left to do. But you would never know it by talking to them.

In the cancer center, all the facades fall away. It's real life to the core. After meeting these amazing warriors, I don't think anyone else will ever really impress me. Most encouraging of all, we even met a few people who had beat leukemia and had a bone marrow transplant and were now thriving.

Sadly, there were also those whose transplant was a few years behind them and they were now dying from the side effects of chemotherapy, radiation and the transplant itself. Cancer doesn't care if you're male, female, an athlete, an infant, a grandpa or a mom. It doesn't care if you are a health food nut or are overweight. It doesn't care if you are rich or poor, what your politics and religion are or where you come from.

It's easy for ignorant but well-meaning people to say the most incredibly insensitive things to people who are going through cancer.

"Hey, eat this or take that vitamin," they say. "I think it will cure you."

But my husband is so sick he can't eat anything but frozen yogurt.

"Is it contagious?"

The only thing that's contagious in this case is ignorance.

Or they might even imply, in the tiniest of ways, that the person somehow deserved to get the cancer because their faith wasn't big enough.

"Or maybe it's their unresolved emotions that caused their cancer."

Whatever it is, I've heard it all! From where I sit, the truth is anyone with cancer has been blindsided. They've done nothing to deserve this living hell.

PARKING ATTENDANTS AND OTHER ANGELS IN DISGUISE

"I'VE SEEN AND MET ANGELS WEARING THE DISGUISE OF OR-
DINARY PEOPLE LIVING ORDINARY LIVES." —TRACY CHAPMAN

I f you make many trips to a hospital, finding a decent parking spot becomes a highlight of your day.

I soon came to rely on the wonderful valet parking attendants at Sacred Heart. I always had my hands full with my
computer bag, purse, phone and charger, snacks, water and fresh
jammies for Chris. So the parking attendants got to know me
and my schedule pretty well.

They were so kind. There was one young man in particular,
also named Chris, who had to be an angel in disguise. He would
always let me park right in front of the entrance.

"Don't worry about it!" He would say with a smile.

He will probably never know how this extra kindness made
all the difference.

Chris would be on the seventh floor or eighth floor, so I usually tried to take the stairs. I did my best to get that little bit of

exercise ,since I would be sitting in a hospital room chair for the majority of the day.

We had our little routines. Chris would order his meals for the day, but after a while he wanted to eat something new. We found I could go downstairs and get a meal coupon to use in the hospital cafeteria instead. So we would look forward to "going out for lunch," which meant a trek down to the hospital cafeteria. I always got the same harvest salad, still one of my favorites. Chris would get a turkey sandwich and his frozen yogurt. There weren't many patients eating in the cafeteria. It was mostly just visitors and hospital staff. Finding a table was never difficult. Once we showed up and people saw that Chris was bald, in a nightgown and attached to a chemo pole with a skull and crossbones, everyone suddenly seemed to be done eating and we always had a free table.

The cancer journey can be a very lonely time. It's easy to feel like no one on the outside understands what you are going through. As I scrolled through Facebook, I saw people complaining because their dog got into the garbage or their haircut didn't turn out just right. These moments were difficult to see for me. I felt like they didn't know what real problems were. But now I realize that we all go through difficult times, maybe not leukemia, but something. We all suffer at one time or another. It's part of the human condition. It was just our season for suffering.

I heard a song the other day that made me think of those parking attendants. I think of all the people who do their job without fame or fortune, yet with pride and excellence. They are truly the people who make the world go round.

Howard drives a minivan with the cruise ships from Ft. Lauderdale

And it's been that way since 1994

Does his business on a flip phone with the most obnoxious ringtone

I didn't ask but I can tell he's from New York

And he spoke proudly of his daughter and that this fall she'd be in college

And that he always wished he'd gotten his degree

You can tell he came from nothing, built a future out of hustling

And somehow I'm the one you people pay to see

Oh isn't that just the way it goes

You're dealt a good hand and you get celebrated

Oh how am I the only one who knows

I'm half the man of the men that drive me places

Danny showed up early fifteen minutes till five thirty

Making sure that I'd be on my morning flight

He said he'd love to fix computers, but that he can't until he's fluent

So he spends his driving money taking class at night

He wore a neatly ironed dress shirt and he helps his kids with homework

And deep inside I couldn't help but ask myself

Why that at night I'm up on stage, everybody knows my name

While Danny's early picking up somebody else

Oh isn't that just the way it goes

You're dealt a good hand and you get celebrated

Oh how am I the only one who knows

I'm half the man of the men that drive me places

And now everything's not given, I work hard to make my living

But I'll give credit where I think credits due

Maybe you got dealt a good hand

Maybe you play it the best that you can

But I don't know how far you'd walk without those cards

In Howard and Danny's working shoes

But that's just the way it goes

You're dealt a good hand and you get celebrated

Oh how am I the only one who knows

I'm half the man of the men that drive me places

The Men That Drive Me Places —Ben Rector

.

YOU DON'T NEED JESUS UNTIL YOU'RE HERE

"GOD GIVES US ONLY WHAT WE CAN HANDLE. APPARENTLY GOD THINKS I'M A BAD-ASS."

Have you ever broken into tears while you're driving? With your tears flowing so fast you can barely see the road?

Well, that was me on a gorgeous fall day I will never forget.

We were on a short car trip to watch Joya sing for a fundraising event. It was a huge deal for her because she was very shy with her singing and was going to sing on stage in front of people. Chris wanted to make sure we were there for her, with him wearing a mask, of course! He was feeling pretty good in-between chemo treatments, so the boys turned this voyage into a little fishing trip. My daughter and her friend and I drove in a separate car. And this song came on. I played it over and over again. And I bawled my eyes out.

Woke up this morning

And I heard the news

I know the pain of a heartbreak, yeah

I don't have answers
And neither do you
I know the pain of a heartbreak

This isn't easy
This isn't clear
And you don't need Jesus
Til you're here
Then confusion and the doubts you had
Up and walk away
They walk away
When a heart breaks

I heard the doctor
But what did he say
I knew I was fine about this time yesterday
I don't need answers
I just need some peace
I just need someone who could help me get some sleep
Who could help me get some sleep

This isn't easy
This isn't clear
And you don't need Jesus
Til you're here
Then confusion and the doubts you had
Up and walk away
They walk away

When a heart breaks

When a Heart Breaks —Ben Rector

The song hit home on so many levels. One day everything is fine and the next day nothing is fine. It can happen that fast. The line "You don't need Jesus, until you're here" could mean a lot of different things. To me it means that when things are going well in life, we usually turn our nose up to the idea of needing a Savior or God because, you know, *we've got this. Life is pretty easy and we are doing just fine by ourselves.*

Yet at the first sign of disaster, what is the first thing people do? Even people who don't believe in God? They pray to him. That's right, now they suddenly need Jesus! Personally, I was extremely grateful that I had called on God so many times in my life that it was second nature to me when Chris got sick to cry out to God for help. Call me nerdy, or a Bible thumper, or Karen (I've been called all the names) but I am content to know and consider the Holy Spirit my best friend and closest companion. As John 14:26 says, "But the Comforter (Counselor, Helper, Intercessor, Advocate, Strengthener, Standby), the Holy Spirit, Whom the Father will send in my name (in my place, to represent me and act on my behalf) He will teach you all things. And He will cause you to recall (will remind you of, bring to your remembrance) everything I have told you."

So friends, don't wait for the ball to drop. Know *whose* you are, know *who* you are and if and when something crazy happens which is life, then you'll have someone to lean on who can actually comfort you and guide you in those crazy times.

PAIN IS JUST WEAKNESS LEAVING THE BODY

"CRAWLING IS ACCEPTABLE, FALLING IS ACCEPTABLE, PUKING IS
ACCEPTABLE, BLOOD IS ACCEPTABLE AND PAIN IS ACCEPTABLE.
QUITTING IS NOT."

One of the things Marines like to say is that pain is just weakness leaving the body. I always thought that was absurd.

Pain is telling you there is a problem!

But the older I get, the more I understand this saying. So much of what we handle and overcome in life is between our ears.

Let me tell you a little bit about the pain that cancer patients go through. There is usually some pain from the cancer itself. In Chris's case, it was severe pain in his hips and head. The rest of the pain comes from the treatments, medications, tests and procedures.

Here's the Mayo Clinic's list of possible side effects from just one of the intravenous chemotherapies used to fight acute lymphoblastic leukemia. Just to show how different it is for different patients, I've put an asterisk next to the ones Chris experienced.

More common

1. blurred or double vision*
2. constipation*
3. difficulty walking*
4. drooping eyelids*
5. headache*
6. jaw pain
7. joint pain*
8. lower back or side pain*
9. numbness or tingling in fingers and toes*
10. pain in fingers and toes
11. pain in testicles
12. stomach cramps
13. swelling of feet or lower legs*
14. weakness*

Less common

1. agitation*
2. bed-wetting* *Does peeing on the floor count?!*
3. confusion*
4. convulsions (seizures)
5. decrease or increase in urination*
6. dizziness or lightheadedness when getting up from a lying or sitting position*
7. hallucinations, or seeing, hearing, or feeling things that are not there* This might explain the time that Chris pointed to the room and told the nurse and me to look at the beautiful neon fireflies. He said he could almost touch them!
8. lack of sweating
9. loss of appetite*
10. mental depression
11. painful or difficult urination
12. trouble in sleeping *** Absolutely. Add prednisone to this and look out! Chris didn't really sleep well for months.
13. unconsciousness

Rare

    1. Sores in mouth and on lips*

Fascinating, right? And remember, that's just one list. Many different drugs were used to combat Chris's leukemia. Here is the WebMD list of side effects of Prednisone, a steroid commonly used during cancer treatment. I've used asterisks to indicate which ones he experienced firsthand.

1. Bone thinning (osteoporosis)
2. Eye problems like glaucoma and cataracts
3. High blood pressure
4. Worsening diabetes (in Chris's case it caused actual diabetes)*
5. Higher risk of infection
6. Increased appetite and weight gain (otherwise known as a steroid belly)*
7. Mood swings *** Um, yes someone should have told us about this one! Think Incredible Hulk when he turned green.
8. Nervousness and restlessness
9. Skin problems like easy bruising and slower wound healing
10. Sleep problems ** What they mean by this one is you won't sleep for six months...
11. Stomach upset (especially if taken with ibuprofen or naproxen)
12. Swollen, puffy face
13. Water retention, swelling in lower legs

Something that is not on this list is when they put you on this long term at high doses, it eats your muscles away.

There were too many medications and too many side effects to list, but this is just a taste of the action. All for a 50/50 shot at surviving.

One of the standard tests frequently done on a leukemia patient is called a lumbar puncture. Here's how Wikipedia explains it:

Lumbar puncture, also known as a spinal tap, is a medical procedure in which a needle is inserted into the spinal canal, most commonly to collect cerebrospinal fluid for diagnostic testing... Increased intracranial pressure is a contraindication, due to risk of brain matter being compressed and pushed toward the spine... Post-dural-puncture headache is a common side effect.

My lucky husband received this fun procedure at least a half dozen times. They do offer some kind of pain medicine to help offset the agony; however, it has to be administered correctly and the timing of the actual puncture needs to be in a certain window while the patient is numb. Unfortunately, more often than not, the timing was off.

One time in particular, as I was sitting outside the sterile room in the hospital hallway waiting for his procedure to be done, I heard him yell out in terrible pain. This is a lot for anyone to deal with, but for someone like Chris who avoided doctors and could barely handle a blood draw because needles made him queasy, this was even more traumatic.

I mentioned the picc line Chris had inserted upon every hospital stay. Wikipedia says this:

A peripherally inserted central catheter, less commonly called a percutaneous indwelling central catheter, is a form of intravenous access that can be used for a prolonged period of time or for administration of substances that should not be done peripherally. It is a catheter that enters the body through the skin at a peripheral site, extends to the superior vena cava, and stays in place for days or weeks.

It's actually a wonderful invention, but not exactly fun to have inserted multiple times. There are also ports that can be inserted for long term chemotherapy, and Chris did eventually graduate to one of these, called a Hickman.

The most painful procedure of all was the bone marrow biopsy. This is where they lay the patient down on a table and use a corkscrew type of tool to drill into the bones. This is done in order to obtain the bone marrow, usually at the hip. I was able to be in the room for one of the times, and even though they do offer medication to the patients, it's the kind that gives you temporary amnesia, not as much preventing the pain. I think of it as the Michael Jackson drug.

The reason I know this is because I watched my husband just about jump off of the operating table when they were corkscrewing into his hip bone, with all of his pain medications on board. Of course, he didn't remember it afterward, but I'll never forget it!

I can't overemphasize how tough my husband was, and how tough all cancer patients have to be to get through their treatments. They have my deepest respect for going through what they do in order to have another chance at living. Chris and every one of these people are all my heroes. Whenever I asked Chris how he dealt with that kind of pain and suffering, he always said the same thing.

"Jesus suffered way more than I am and he will never give me more than I can handle."

Romans 5:3 echoes that thought. "But that's not all! Even in times of trouble we have a joyful confidence, knowing that our pressures will develop in us patient endurance."

I can't comprehend what the families of a child who has cancer must go through. We have a good friend who is also a cancer survivor, against all odds, and he has a fitting name for these patients, their family and their caregivers.

Cancer warriors.

Yes, they truly arc.

NOT EVEN THE KING

"A MAN'S DAUGHTER IS HIS HEART. JUST WITH FEET, WALKING
OUT IN THE WORLD." —MAT JOHNSON

W e were about halfway through the initial phase of Chris's cancer treatment. He had been hospitalized at least seven times for a week minimum in order to get his chemotherapy infusions. Sometimes his body would bounce back quickly and sometimes more slowly. At those times we would wait to start the treatment. The whole time we tiptoed through life with the hope that he wouldn't come down with a simple cold or anything else, since he had very little ability to fight off even the simplest of viruses. Even one of these could derail his lifesaving treatment and the leukemia might have time to come back with a vengeance.

While she was bored at home, Joya had been working on a special surprise for her dad. She loved to sing and was learning to play the guitar. She has the most beautiful, unique voice. But she was also extremely shy about performing and did not want to put herself out there. She would have never considered posting her singing on social media or anything like that.

But this particular year, month, song and moment was different. She wanted to do something extra special for her dad. She knew how much he loved to hear her sing. So one day while we were at the hospital yet again, she propped up her cell phone to record her, kneeling on the bathroom floor (great acoustics!).

"This is for you, Daddy," she said.

And then she sang a lovely song in her loveliest voice. And she posted it to YouTube, overcoming her shyness and self-doubt, so her daddy in his hospital could hear her sing.

Money

Some people so poor, all that they've got is money

Oh, and diamonds

Some people waste their life counting their thousands

I don't care what they're offering

How much gold they bring

They can't afford what we've had

Not even the king

They can't afford what we've got

Not even the king

Oh, castles

Some people so lonely, what good is a castle

Surrounded by people?

But ain't got a friend that's not on the payroll

Oh, and I don't care what they bring

They can have everything

They can't afford what we've got

Not even the king

They can't afford what we've got

Not even the king

All the king's horses and all the king's men
Came charging to get what we got
They offered the crown and they offered the throne
I already got what I want

All the king's horses and all the king's men
They came marching through
They offered the world just to have what we got
But I found the world in you
I found the world in you

So darling, listen (except she sang so daddy, listen)
Your arms around me worth more than a kingdom
Yeah, believe that
The trust that we feel the kings never felt that

Yeah, this is the song that we sing
We don't need anything
They can't afford this
This is priceless

Can't afford what we've got
Not even the king
Can't afford what we've got
Not even the king

Not Even the King—Alicia Keys

I was with Chris when he watched the video for the first time, and it was incredible. While he watched Joya sing, tears welled up in his eyes and he got that cute little grin that he gets when he's happy and trying at the same time not to let the tears of joy fall freely.

Let me tell you, friends, only the most difficult of times can make a moment as precious as this.

Yes, we still have some bad memories about this time in our lives, but for every bad memory, we have many more precious, amazing memories like these. Our family gave everything we could to help our husband and daddy get better, knowing full well we had no guarantee. We chose to put our trust in God, whether he took Chris home to be with him forever or gave him a second chance. We clung to the promise.

His best days were ahead of him.

Trusting God meant that we had to silence the other voices in our heads and believe me, they were many, and sometimes they were loud. Philippians 4:8 says, "So keep your thoughts continually fixed on all that is authentic and real, honorable and admirable, beautiful and respectful, pure and holy, merciful and kind. And fasten your thoughts on every glorious work of God, praising him always."

So how does that look in real life? We tried our best to look for the good in every situation. We were thankful for the excellent medical care we got. (Even when there were medical mistakes made, and they do happen. Have you ever wondered why doctors are called practicing physicians?)

Good things do come out of the worst of circumstances. And laughter. The funny moments are definitely there in the cancer journey, if you're ready for them. I mean, what's funnier than a hairless (not just bald like in the movies) man throwing up in a McDonalds drive through? Yes, that happened.

You really can't afford to take life too seriously because guess what? We're all going to die! That's right! So let's live! Let's put our trust in Almighty God and live!

That attitude is something wonderful Chris taught me. And he taught me how to laugh. I'm the most serious and literal human on the planet. But living with Chris Harper for almost 30 years has taught me how to joke around and find the humor in everything.

Life is meant to be lived and celebrated and humor always helps. Like the time when we went to visit Chris in the hospital and he called down to the cafeteria and ordered a bunch of fruit plates for us. The nurse came in and asked, "Is there anything else I can get for you guys, maybe some fruit?" We all busted out laughing.

Looking back now, I can honestly say that we had some of our best and closest family moments during this trying time. So like the song says, you're only poor if you don't have those close relationships. What good is living in a mansion with no one to love? A hug can mean more than a kingdom.

Our tight knit family became a gift so rare not even a king could afford.

Joya's lovely version of the song. is on YouTube as Not Even The King Alicia Keys Cover

CHRIS HARPER
OBITUARY

"TRULY I TELL YOU, IF YOU HAVE FAITH AS SMALL AS A MUS-
TARD SEED, YOU CAN SAY TO THIS MOUNTAIN MOVE FROM
HERE TO THERE AND IT WILL MOVE. NOTHING WILL BE IMPOS-
SIBLE FOR YOU." —JESUS

And then the strangest thing happened.

Chris and I went out to breakfast on one of his "good" days. One of the things that was heavy on his mind was his upcoming bone marrow transplant. He felt very conflicted about going forward with the treatment. First, because he was finally getting to a point where he felt pretty good most days. And second, the descriptions we'd heard of the process were terrifying.

Every day we prayed for guidance.

Should we go forward with the bone marrow transplant? All signs seemed to point in that direction. And from what we understood, didn't have much of a choice if Chris wanted to live.

Once we were seated and the waitress poured our coffee, Chris picked up the local newspaper sitting on our table. It happened to be open to the obituary section. He looked at me wide-eyed and pointed to one of the names.

Christopher Harper, the obituary said. *Age 45.*

We both did a double take to make sure we weren't both seeing things. My Chris's official name was Christopher, and he was also 45.

This couldn't be real.

As we read on, things became even more eerie. This stranger with my husband's name and same age had died from complications from pneumonia *after* surviving acute lymphoblastic leukemia and a bone marrow transplant.

What did it mean? What are the odds that these two men would share such similarities, that the obituary would run, that we would happen to see it at breakfast?

Was this a sign? Should we not do the transplant?

So many thoughts ran through our head at that moment that time seemed to stop.

It was a stark reminder. Just because someone gets a bone marrow transplant, it's not always a happy ending. Half of all the people will die from a complication. Even if the BMT cures the cancer, the chemotherapy and radiation can cause secondary cancers and compromised health, sometimes for many years. Or the immune-suppressing drugs can allow something like pneumonia to deliver the killer blow instead. Yet another outcome can be terrible reactions from graft versus host disease. The donor cells and the host cells cannot co-exist, and a difficult life or a painful death can follow.

So we were trapped in a terrible dilemma. Did Chris want to go through grueling treatment with a 50/50 chance at beating an awful disease, just so the treatment itself might kill him?

It would take all the faith we could possibly muster to move forward with the transplant.

One day when I meet my maker, I'm going to ask Him if that obituary article was a real thing or was it something put in our path to cause us to stumble? It's a crazy thought, but who knows?

For now, I take comfort in 1 Cor 13:12. "For now we see only a reflection as in a mirror. Then we shall see face to face. Now I know in part. Then I shall know fully, even as I am fully known."

A BRAIN FULL
OF CHEMO

"ALTHOUGH THE WORLD IS FULL OF SUFFERING, IT IS ALSO
FULL OF THE OVERCOMING OF IT." —HELEN KELLER

I t had been a few months now since Chris's diagnosis. We'd gotten through the tough winter and were headed into the optimism of spring. We were about two-thirds done with the initial chemo treatments and Chris's doctor believed he was in remission.

That is until that fateful spring day I left Chris at home to rest while I took Jared to his nearby weekend baseball tournament where he was the starting pitcher.

"Call me when you wake up," I told Chris. "I'll come and get you for one of the games if you feel up to it."

I was doing all of the driving again these days. Chris didn't feel strong enough. The chemo treatments were really taking their toll on him and he wasn't bouncing back as quickly as he had in the early stages of treatment. His big activity of the day was walking to the mailbox, which he would do when he felt a boost of energy from one of his many blood transfusions.

When Chris finally did call me at the baseball game, his voice sounded strange.

"I think I'm having a stroke," he said. "I need you to drive me to the hospital."

I asked a friend to look after Jared and drive him home. I tried to downplay the seriousness of the situation. The poor kid was only 11, very competitive, and already putting intense pressure on himself if he didn't pitch a perfect game. So the added pressure of having a sick dad took its toll.

I called Chris's oncologist on his cell phone.

"Get him straight to the hospital," he said.

It was heart-wrenching to see my husband in this condition after everything he'd been through. One of his eyelids was drooping and he told me he had a horrible headache.

He greeted us at the hospital entrance with everything in place for Chris to be admitted. Problem was, the ER department felt like they had to do their due diligence, so we waited for hours in a small room while they ran tests. This is even though Chris's oncologist was ready and waiting for him to be admitted upstairs on the cancer floor.

So frustrating!

It wasn't a stroke. Rather, he had these strange neurological symptoms that they couldn't diagnose without further testing. *I could have told them that!*

After several MRIs and other tests, they decided to try a blood patch to treat his intense headache. They had no explanation for the drooping eye at this point other than they thought one of the lumbar punctures might have created a small hole in his spinal cord.

What?!

We were about to learn yet another medical procedure. Here are a few juicy tidbits from Wikipedia's description:

An epidural blood patch is a surgical procedure that uses autologous blood in order to close one or many holes in the dura mater of the spinal cord, usually as a result of a previous lumbar puncture. A small amount of the patient's blood is injected into the epidural space near the site of the original puncture; the resulting blood clot then "patches" the meningeal leak. The procedure carries the typical risks of any epidural puncture. However, even though it is often effective, further intervention is sometimes necessary.

After the blood patch, Chris's headache eased a little. So he sweet-talked his doctor into releasing him from the hospital. Did I mention he was a great salesman? Unfortunately, it wasn't a long term fix, and the headache came back with a vengeance.

By now, we had the kids loaded up and were on our way to Seattle for our initial consultation for the bone marrow transplant procedure. The five-hour drive seemed like five days. Chris's head was hurting so bad that even if one of us chewed our gum or breathed it was amplified in his skull and he yelled out in pain.

We finally got checked into our room, which my aunt who lived in the Seattle area had arranged for us. What a blessing. I don't know how I could have even handled reserving a room at that point. She put us up at this amazing place called the Seattle Cancer Care Alliance House. It's reserved for cancer patients and their families who are undergoing cancer treatments. It is extra clean and quiet. Not only did she get us two rooms so our big family could be comfortable, she also stocked both mini kitchens full of the best organic food that money could buy.

I took one look at all that healthy food and broke down sobbing. I wept tears of pure relief and joy. It's impossible to describe how her kindness touched us. The kids were happier than I had seen in months. It sounds like such a simple thing, but they hadn't had a home-cooked meal in ages. When they saw all of the delicious, healthy food available for them, they were ecstatic.

I tucked Chris into bed after many trips to the bathroom for his vomiting, made sure the kids were comfortable and tried to get some sleep for the big day. I was already exhausted, and I knew it would be a big day tomorrow.

And boy, was it ever. We sat through hours and hours of question and answer sessions, along with medical tests to get Chris prepared for his bone marrow transplant. There was the huge task of finding a match, along with information overload. Chris couldn't concentrate at all during our question-and-answer session with the doctor due to his raging migraine and violent vomiting.

Here we faced all those ugly facts that you do not want to hear about a bone marrow transplant. There was the mini version and the full transplant, and in his case, the doctors recommended the full transplant. Apparently most people are able to get the mini these days, but he would not be so lucky. The full transplant protocol included extremely high doses of more chemo, followed by total body radiation, with an extra shot of radiation to his head and testicles, followed by the bone marrow transplant itself. He would then require 100 days of close monitoring before he could go home. As before, we were told Chris had a 10 percent chance of long-term survival, meaning five years or more, without the transplant, and a 50 percent chance of long-term survival with the transplant. This is because the chemotherapy cocktail, along with the total body radiation to kill the leukemia cells, would also kill his good bone marrow cells. These cells would no longer be capable of making red blood cells, platelets or white blood cells. If the transplant didn't take then Chris would die.

Frightening odds, but there it was. We had to take our chances and move forward. We couldn't go on like this.

His treatments would happen at Seattle Cancer Care Alliance, in partnership with University of Washington Medical Center and Fred Hutchinson Cancer Research Center. These specialists from all over the world know cancer and bone marrow transplants inside and out. We would be working with the doctors and nurses on what they called the Tan Team. The facility used colors to designate groups of specialists who worked together. They alternated doctors and the whole team would treat him.

While we were in Seattle we celebrated Jared's birthday at iFly Indoor Skydiving. We tried our best to make this medical trip into a family outing, and even though this was excruciating for Chris, he sucked it up so the kids could have a little fun.

During the endless ride home we had to remain completely silent. His migraine was out of control. Time for yet another call to his doctor and yet another ER visit and hospital stay.

How much could one man take?

His neurological symptoms worsened. The whole side of his face became virtually useless. He had to lift his eyelid with his other hand in order to see.

This time the doctor decided he saw some suspicious activity on the MRI involving the optic nerve in Chris's brain. Next thing we knew, Chris had brain surgery.

The doctors installed a device into his brain called an Ommaya reservoir. When he came out of surgery he looked like Frankenstein, with a big lump on the front of his head and a row of bloody staples.

The surgery had gone fine. But there was a frightening red flag.

"We've taken another sample of his cerebrospinal fluid during surgery," the oncologist said. "I'm concerned it may test positive for leukemia in the brain."

What?! How much more can we take?

The oncologist promised me by 9 p.m. that day he would let us know the official results. That was the longest day of my life, and 9 p.m. came and went with no news. Finally, I'm ashamed to say, I lost my mind and lit into the head nurse on duty. She was so patient and kind, even in the face of my impatience, and was able to reach our doctor (perhaps by dragging him out of bed). Finally he was at the hospital giving us the dreaded diagnosis face-to-face.

"The MRI results showing the activity on Chris's optic nerve, along with his neurological symptoms and the test of his cerebrospinal fluid, are all leading to the diagnosis of leukemia in the brain," he said.

Those were terrifying words. And this latest turn was very hard on our morale.

Compared to this, Chris had pretty much sailed through the chemo. Yes, he lost his hair (all over his entire body, not like the movies where they still have long eyelashes and eyebrows). Yes, throwing up was a daily activity. Yes he was tired, but he still functioned somewhat normally. He still went to the kid's activities and ran our business. He was still a participant in the game of life. All that changed with this new diagnosis.

The next morning before I arrived at the hospital, Chris cornered his oncologist and asked him to level with him.

"What are my chances now?" Chris asked.

The oncologist paused, and the look on his face told Chris everything he needed to know. It was the first time he'd seen this confident doctor look nervous and uncertain.

"We're going to throw absolutely everything we can at it," the doctor said. "We need to knock the hell out of this thing. But I'm going to warn you, this will be the hardest thing you have ever done."

The new treatment plan was to stick a needle into the Ommaya reservoir, then drip a new chemo cocktail directly into Chris's brain. The cocktail consisted of two different types of chemotherapy drugs along with a steroid. The first time the oncologist administered this cocktail, Chris became violently sick for what seemed like an eternity. I mean it when I say violently sick. I think the doctor was even surprised by the violent eruption. He sat alongside the hospital bed and rubbed Chris's back for what seemed like hours. Chris said he could hear the liquid chemo dripping into his brain, sort of like the sound of pouring paint into a paint can.

Drip, drip drip.

After a few of these treatments, some of which could be done in the doctor's office rather than in the hospital his neurological symptoms started improving. One of the reasons the Ommaya reservoir was implanted into his brain was to avoid those painful lumbar punctures. Now the cerebrospinal fluid could be drawn out through the Ommaya (virtually painless, I was assured). And the chemotherapy to kill leukemia cells in his brain could be administered the same way fluid was withdrawn, through a needle into the Ommaya reservoir. I can tell you that when Chris got this treatment in the doctor's office, I'm pretty sure he cleared a few waiting rooms with the loud sounds of violent puking. It wasn't good for business, that I am sure of.

We all thought we were on the right path. The nurses and

CNAs were absolute Godsends. So very good at their jobs, so kind and always going above and beyond their job descriptions.

There was only one nurse throughout our entire ordeal that left a negative impression. I'm sure she meant well, but she came into Chris's room after his brain surgery and the initial brain leukemia diagnosis and said something very odd:

"How are you both dealing with this bad news?"

Chris and I looked at each other, and I kid you not, I had a Saturday Night Live-style comedy skit run through my mind of lunging across the room at her and choking her out.

How do you think we are dealing? We were just told that my husband now had brain cancer!

Something about her bedside manner that made me want to puke. I counted the hours until her shift was over.

Maybe it was how she pitied us. Maybe that made it all seem more real.

One day Chris just decided, without saying anything to me, that he would ride his four-wheeler off into the woods, just to blow off steam. He did take Josh with him.

At this point my husband had a black eye patch over his droopy eye and was carved up like Frankenstein. What was worse, he somehow managed to climb a tree.

"I wanted to get my trail cam back before I lost it," he said in his defense as I shook my head. Only a diehard hunter would understand.

"Well, I'm not happy with you OR my son," I said. "In your weakened state, that was dangerous to say the least."

But what are you going to do? He'd had the best day ever that day.

You just can't keep a good man down. I heard him answer his phone, right in the middle of throwing up, just to answer his calls to keep our business running. I saw him sitting through three baseball games in a row while toughing it out through a horrific migraine. I gained more respect for Chris watching him navigate cancer than at any other time in our lives.

Our newest treatment plan consisted of alternating week-long hospitalized chemo treatments followed by chemo treatments in his brain. The goal was 16 rounds of this.

And here's where our summer really went to hell in a hand-basket. Chris started acting really mentally slow. Giant drops of sweat poured from his head onto his pillow, which smelled like a toxic plastic factory. It had to be the excess chemo, trying to find a way out of his body.

I was always on a knife's edge during this time. Chris was trying to rest while we had a houseful of kids, being noisy like kids do. His brain was full of chemo. It was the perfect storm.

THE CAMPING TRIP FROM HELL

"YOU WILL NEVER KNOW THE VALUE OF A MOMENT UNTIL IT
BECOMES A MEMORY." —DR SEUSS

I n the midst of all the medical chaos, Chris pushed to have a family camping trip. He can be very convincing. He later told me he thought this might be his last trip with us. With so much stacked against us, we were doing our best to believe. But in the back of our minds a small dark thought would tell us otherwise.

So we did it. We packed up our motorhome, fishing boat, ski boat, a tent, tons of food, our two dogs and off we went. It was quite the Harper family caravan. Jordan was driving one vehicle and towing a boat, Josh was driving another vehicle and towing the other boat. I had to drive the motorhome. Chris wanted to drive but couldn't see out of one of his eyes. I'd always teased him that he wasn't a good driver anyway.

"Honey, with only one seeing eye, I can only imagine how many mailboxes you would have taken out just leaving our neighborhood," I tried to tease him.

It was such a different experience than our past trips. Usually Chris was the one who set up camp, gathered firewood, cooked the food and entertained the family, whether driving the boat or telling jokes and stories. This time those jobs fell on Josh's shoulders and mine.

Camping was not the same. It was a lot of work!

We were used to showing up, having fun then going home. Now there was packing and unpacking, cooking, cleaning and organizing. Chris rested in the motorhome most of the time, racked with headache after headache. He gobbled pain pills, anti-nausea pills and anti-anxiety pills. I was torn between going out on the boats with the kids to have a little fun, or staying in the motorhome to keep a close eye on Chris. I was pretty worried about him.

We sat silently around the fire at night and I knew what we were thinking about. Nobody said it but we could all see how Chris was declining, both mentally and physically. He continued to act mentally slower. He started to seem unengaged from reality. I convinced myself it was one of the many side effects of either the cancer itself (God forbid could it be spreading even further) or the treatment for the cancer. So I did what I did best in those dark days. I slapped a smile on my face for the kids and to inspire Chris and I held it inside.

It was a short campout because we were due for yet another brain chemo session. Each time we had a looming appointment, the anxiety levels started to rise in all of us. It was a huge ordeal. The doctor tried without success to figure out a way to administer the treatment without making Chris ill.

And so the dreaded routine began again. First Chris would get situated In a chemo chair. Then they would start his IV. They would pump him full of IV fluids and liquid Ativan, an anti-nausea and anti-anxiety medication that cancer patients eat like candy. Once he was nice and comfy they would take him to a private room. There the oncologist would administer the drugs with a small needle inserted into the Omaya reservoir implanted in his brain. Then we would wait for the puking to begin. Like clockwork it would start soon thereafter and continue until Chris had nothing left to give. Then we would sheepishly get in the car and go home to rest. This process continued 16 times.

Sadly, the longer the treatment went on, the less I recognized my husband.

RUNNING AWAY

"MAY I NEVER FORGET, ON MY BEST DAY, THAT I NEED GOD AS
DESPERATELY AS I DID ON MY WORST DAY." —MIKE EPPS

Days and nights went by in a blur, while we did what we were supposed to do to fight this cancer by showing up to every single appointment. But now, when I would call Chris's name, he would respond as if in slow motion. It scared me to think I might be losing him.

Then things took a drastic turn.

I knew Chris was resting, but I came to talk to him about something the kids needed.

"Be quiet," he said.

I thought that was rude and I just kept talking.

Next thing I knew he flew into a rage the likes of which I had never seen. He erupted from the bed. He punched the bedroom door. Then he began flinging dresser drawers. Imagine the incredible Hulk throwing a tantrum, but in slow motion.

It must have been the steroids. He was on some very heavy doses. The thought that it might affect his behavior this badly had never crossed my mind.

I remember being so incredibly scared. My two middle sons were home at the time and ran to the bedroom doorway to see what the ruckus was. I grabbed the back of both their shirts (one of them was over 200 pounds) and jerked them out of the house, into the garage and into my car. We drove away.

That was the worst moment of my life. I probably could have handled it better, but I had to get away. He's a very strong man, even when weakened by cancer. Out of his mind, high on the chemicals, I had no idea what he might do.

I called Josh, bawling into the phone, while the boys and I drove around the neighborhood trying to figure out what to do. Josh sped home to help. He got there just in time to see his dad pulling out of the driveway. Chris had absolutely no business behind the wheel. He couldn't see out of one eye, was mentally slow and hadn't been driving for months. Josh tried to stop him. He outran Josh by speeding away and disappeared around the corner.

I was a wreck. Somewhere out there, was my husband, out of his mind, weak, tired, seeing out of one eye. He wasn't answering his phone. He'd left his medications behind.

We called his best friend and he convinced us to call the police. The kids and I split up and drove around trying to find him. The kids were freaking out. Jared wanted to jump out of the car because he didn't feel that his daddy loved him anymore. Josh, on the other hand, wanted to find his dad and then fistfight him for all the chaos he was causing. Joya and Jordan just tried to help with the search. I couldn't relate to what he was going through and I didn't have much sympathy for him at this moment. We kept calling him and leaving messages, not realizing that he'd left his phone at home.

A couple hours into our search, I had got a voicemail from him. He'd apparently bought a tracfone so that we couldn't trace him. I guess his Marine Corp skills came in handy that night.

"I just can't take it anymore," his message said. "I'm going to be in the woods for a couple of weeks to a couple of months. Tell my doctor to pound sand. I'm not going to have any more chemo dumped into my brain."

He also told me he wanted a divorce, which really stung. I now know that this was his dysfunctional way of not wanting to put me through anymore of this.

One moment I was so angry with him. *How could he do this to us? The kids were beside themselves!* Then two seconds later my heart would go out to him. *I miss him. I'm so worried about him. Will we ever find him? Or will he stumble around in the woods and freeze overnight? He's in no condition to be out anywhere. It's pouring rain and he's weak, cold, wet and tired.*

The cops asked if I wanted to file a missing persons report. I decided to wait it out overnight and see what the morning brought. When I went to bed that night, I said a prayer for my runaway husband. *Lord, he is your problem tonight. Please be with him, keep him safe, let him be okay. In Jesus name, Amen.*

There was nothing else I could do. So I rolled over, completely at peace, and went to sleep. I knew somehow that God was watching over him and that everything would be fine.

That night I had the strangest dream. I dreamed that I was the one with the cancer in my brain. The dream was so real. When I awoke I had nothing but compassion in my heart for him.

That next morning, I called his oncologist.

"Is it okay that Chris has run away in his current condition and is somewhere lost in the woods?" I asked him.

"No!" the doctor barked in his Croatian accent, "It is not okay. We need to f**ing find him immediately and get him to the hospital."

I then called the police to go ahead and file the missing persons report. This way they could actually look for him and safely bring him in. Without this, he was just some guy who'd just decided he wanted to get away from his home life.

As soon as I hung up with the police, my phone rang. It was Chris. He didn't say much, only that he was coming home. I cancelled the missing persons request and waited for my husband. He drove up, got out of the car, stumbled into the house, went straight to bed and slept until I woke him for the ride to the hospital. This time, he went compliantly, knowing he wasn't really going to stop the chemo, knowing he did want to survive and get better.

In case you are wondering where he really went that night, he went shopping at Walmart in a small town toward Canada (in his mind he was going to go to Canada) and attempted to buy fishing supplies and camping gear. He must've looked pretty crazy in his condition because people kept looking at him and asking him if he was okay.

Then he looked outside, saw the pouring rain, ditched his basket full of supplies and went to the nearest hotel for a good night's rest. The poor guy just needed some peace and quiet. He probably never should have been at home in his current state in the first place. *Hindsight is 20/20!*

This trip to the hospital was much more somber. I think Chris knew that this time he wasn't going to be able to sweet talk his doctor into letting him out early. We checked him in, and the doctor met us in his room. Yet another round of chemo began. This time the doctor and I talked about keeping him in the hospital as long as possible. No getting out early for good behavior. Chris needed care, rest and sleep. The three things he wasn't getting enough of in the midst of a bustling summertime household. And truthfully, I needed a break, too.

This hospital stay lasted about three weeks. Thankfully he got a slight fever, which enabled the doctor to keep him in the hospital. I was so relieved. We could be normal at home and he could be a cancer patient at the hospital, getting the care he needed. I didn't miss a single day of visiting while Chris was hospitalized that dozen times or so. Not one single day. I mainly watched him sleep, but on occasion we would walk the halls or talk, listen to Christian music or cry together.

That night he ran away could've gone so differently. He could easily have gotten into a car accident. I could have decided I'd had enough. The kids could have done something stupid out of confusion and frustration. Chris could have hurt himself or one of us. God was definitely with us all that night.

We knew we were getting close to going to Seattle for his bone marrow transplant. So I put a call into the doctors there for advice regarding chemo and Chris's brain. They agreed that he had had more than enough, so they advised stopping the brain chemo treatments.

Not long before this, they'd tested both of Chris's brothers, who at this point were both supportive of Chris and his treatment, to see if either of them were a match to donate their bone marrow to Chris. There's a 25 percent chance that a sibling will be a match. In our case, neither brother matched. So then they put Chris's blood, DNA and immunity profile out into the network of bone marrow donors to see if they could find a match.

Within two weeks, we had five perfect matches to choose from. If you are reading this, please get on the registry as a potential donor at bethematch.org.

At that point, the scientists at SCCA in Seattle ran a few more tests to see which of the five matched Chris's blood the closest. Much like the case of an organ transplant, the body will try to reject the donated marrow. That's why matching is so important.

We had our match! Due to privacy, they couldn't give us many details, but we did know the blood samples would be coming from a 25-year-old European male. An incredible hero, I'd say.

One day I hope to meet this selfless young man. He can't possibly understand what his gift meant to us. How do you thank someone who gave your husband a new shot at life? A simple thank you is just not enough. I'm sure it was incredibly inconvenient for this young man, missing work, spending countless hours in a clinic somewhere. Not to mention possibly painful, at least to some extent. He could've easily refused to give his stem cells when called upon, but he said yes.

Things went pretty quickly from here. We received phone calls from the team in Seattle, preparing us for our upcoming procedure. We had a date on the calendar to go to Seattle. It was almost time and it couldn't be a moment too soon.

DO YOU TRUST ME?

"PUT ON YOUR BIG GIRL PANTIES AND DEAL WITH IT."

Once again, I was lying in bed praying to Jesus for help.

It seemed to happen a lot these days.

This time I was praying about where my family was going to live. We needed to live in Seattle for the next 100 or so days while Chris received his bone marrow transplant. And we had to be within a certain miles radius from the medical center.

There wasn't much in the way of availability and low cost housing that fit the criteria. We were on a waiting list for a special apartment specifically for cancer families, but last I'd checked, we were still ninth on the list. It had to be an extremely clean place. Hotels aren't known for being germless or conducive for families in general for long periods of time.

And where the kids would go to school? I didn't want to be at the hospital trying to focus on Chris and yet worrying about the kids. I'm certainly a worrywart by nature, so putting all my trust in God was difficult. But little by little, this cancer journey was teaching me to do exactly that. I felt God's presence so much during this season of my life. And I learned to trust Him during even the most difficult of circumstances.

Those days, when I felt that familiar unease in the pit in my stomach, I prayed. And that's exactly what I was doing now.

Lord, please help us find the perfect place to stay and please give me and our family peace.

That's when I heard His voice.

Do you trust me?

Again, this wasn't audible but I clearly heard it. I knew it was Jesus. His voice sounded like velvet and immediately comforted me to my core.

Of course I trust you, Lord, I thought. *Well there was my answer to prayer. God had this. Just like he had every other detail of this journey figured out. I could truly trust Him. I didn't need to worry about where we were going to live and go to school during this time. I only had to trust Him.*

Once again I slept like a baby, knowing God was one step ahead, that He promised to never leave us or forsake us.

Of course, with four kids no day is ever uneventful and the very next day was no different. Jared asked to go motorcycle riding with friends and I agreed. Since he hadn't had much fun lately, it would be one last ride before we left.

Of course, on that one last ride, he broke his knee and was put into a cast for months, just before our road trip to Seattle.

With the Harper family, it was never a dull moment.

SAYING GOODBYE

"DON'T LOOK BACK, YOU'RE NOT GOING THAT WAY."

This was the big day.

We loaded up the car and said goodbye to our home, our eldest son, our dogs and friends.

Take one car, five hours, three kids (one with a cast). Then add a grumpy, tired cancer patient to the mix. Sit back and watch the show.

Actually, I think now that Jared breaking his leg was a blessing in disguise. I'd fretted endlessly about how we were going to keep Jared occupied while living in a downtown apartment or hotel during Chris's treatment. He was such a rambunctious pre-teen. He played year-round sports and never once sat still. But after he broke his leg, he had no choice but to quietly sit and play video games (yes, we bribed him with a new PlayStation) and other apartment-style living activities. The broken leg kept him idle for a period of time which made things strangely calm.

Seattle traffic was terrible and we had no idea where we were going. For now we were headed to a hotel on the outskirts of Seattle until we could find better housing. I remember checking in to our hotel and looking around the lobby. There were lots of strangers, and I felt uneasy about the prospect of this being our kids' home.

Please, God, I whispered under my breath. *Help us find better housing!*

People have told me there's no way they could leave their pet behind for something like this. Yes, you could, I tell them. Because when it comes down to your loved one's survival, things like houses, pets, friends, and stuff being left behind temporarily don't even matter. And I loved my little yorkie, Oscar. My little buddy and emotional support animal. We had to make those hard choices. Due to concerns with germs, pets aren't allowed in the special housing for bone marrow transplant patients. Besides Oscar, we had to leave behind the other comforts of home: privacy, friends, teachers, coaches, entire sports seasons, senior year festivities, homecoming dances, girlfriends and boyfriends, our other son/brother and much more.

In regards to work, I had to leave behind things I took for granted: my desk, a copier, a scanner, file cabinets and other things that helped me do my job with ease and confidence. At this point I wasn't sure if I could continue working remotely, so I filed the necessary paperwork for the Family and Medical Leave Act. Secretly, though, I hoped I could continue to work. My job gave me purpose and it gave me sanity. I'd find a way to get minutes and hours I needed to get the job done. In the end, I'm pleased to say I was able to work the entire time we were in Seattle, surprising not only myself but my bosses, too.

In the end, only two available options would work for our family and qualify for a clean healthy environment close enough to the hospital. The Seattle Cancer Care Alliance House that we had stayed at earlier and the Pete Gross House. Both were extra-clean environments, very near the outpatient clinic for bone marrow transplant patients and hospital. The SCCA house had a community kitchen, so I wasn't sure how well that would go over with the kids. It also had smaller rooms like hotel rooms. We would need a couple of rooms for the size of our family so we would not all be together, therefore costing more money.

The Pete Gross house was an apartment that had the special cancer family Hutch School on the ground floor. Once we were settled at the hotel, I put yet another call into the front desk of the Pete Gross house to let them know we had arrived in Seattle.

"It's go time," I said. "We're here and we're hoping to get an apartment. Can you tell me where we are on the waiting list?"

"Just a minute," she said. "Harper… Hmmm. I'm sorry to say, you're not anywhere on the list."

"What?" I tried to choke down the panic rising in my throat. "But we've been on that list for months, and I've kept checking in to see where we are."

I felt like crying.

And then I remembered those sweet words again.

"Do you trust me?"

Yes, Lord, I do.

I waited.

I prayed.

"Let me call you first thing in the morning," the lady said. "I have the feeling I might have an opening for you".

THE PETE GROSS HOUSE AND HUTCH SCHOOL

"LIFE BEGINS AT THE END OF YOUR COMFORT ZONE."

A t 8:30 the next morning my cell phone rang.

"Good morning," said the lady on the other end of the line. "I'm calling to let you know that if you want an apartment at the Pete Gross House, you have 30 minutes to show up and claim it."

"Yes we do!" I said. "We are on our way right now."

We packed up in a hurry and headed to downtown Seattle.

Thank you, God I! I'm not sure how we went from ninth on the list, to not on the list, to getting an apartment, but I'm not going to argue.

I was instantly at peace, knowing we would be living in a clean apartment close to the hospital and cancer center and that my children would be able to go down the elevator to their day at school and back up again. If I was stuck at the hospital I knew my two teenagers and pre-teen could handle things together until I got home.

The Pete Gross House was an absolute Godsend, is a comfortable, supportive community for patients like Chris and their families who need isolation after transplant. It's located a half-mile from the Seattle Cancer Care Alliance outpatient clinic on Lake Union with shuttle service for patients and family members. Our apartment was furnished and we had a washer, dryer, dishwasher, microwave, range, television, DVD player, linens, and a fully equipped kitchen with a full-size refrigerator. We stayed on the sixth floor.

It was amazing that Jared, Joya and Jordan could commute to school by elevator. The Hutch School is a public school with around 23 students in pre-kindergarten through 12th. There were three teachers, one for elementary, one for middle school and one for high school.

As much as my kids complained about going to a new school and leaving their friends behind, they got some amazing one-on-one teaching during this period. With the teacher-to-student ratio so small, they got special attention. They also became involved with a local Seattle kids poetry writing group, mainly consisting of kids with sickle cell anemia. There were some special field trips like the one to the Mariners baseball game, where we got to meet some of the players and enjoy the game from box seats. (Chris didn't get to go because he was in the hospital). There was a special camaraderie, since everyone in Hutch School understood what the others were going through. Someone in their family was also battling cancer or had cancer themselves. It was a free and accessible public school and I will forever be grateful for it. As I stayed by my husband's side while he battled this terrible disease, my children continued to learn and be supported.

They even offered counseling once a week. Joya really appreciated this aspect of school. It really helped her to be able to talk out some of her fears and concerns. It was a different story for the boys. In their case, counseling seemed to make things worse. At one point I had to ask the principal to please lay off counseling of the boys. For them, it was a constant reminder that they were different and were going through something terrible, as if their daily lives didn't remind them enough.

But how awesome that counseling was. And how incredible the teachers were and how emotionally supportive. They understood if the kids weren't super engaged that day because of something they were going through at home. It was also great for the kids to meet new friends who also could understand what they were going through. Everyone knew why they were there: the C word. They didn't have to feel weird at this school. Everyone had cancer in common. The hardest part was when a new friend had to move away, either because their family member had recovered and they were leaving Seattle or that their family member had passed away and they were leaving Seattle.

The apartment itself was a two-bedroom, so Joya got a room and Chris and I got a room. The two boys shared the pullout couch. There was construction going on all around us so the noise was constant. If it wasn't the construction noise, then it was the police sirens, since we were located in between several halfway houses and quite a large homeless population. It was an eye opener for the kids who were raised in small town USA. In Seattle, we would drive to the grocery store and would go past homeless men and their dogs. Jared would shout out from the back seat, "Mom, I know that guy. That's Big Joe and his dog's name is Bojangles."

This was a bit unnerving to me, the overprotective mama, but the kids reassured me that they were very supervised at recess time, which consisted of playing in the park a few blocks from the Hutch School where a lot of the homeless hung out.

This was all such heavy stuff. My children had to deal with this while their friends at home were playing at their football games and going to their highschool dances. It breaks my heart to think about it. I'm so proud of my kids. They went through all of this without missing a beat. They still graduated on time, continued to do well in their activities and flourished in spite of whatever cancer tried to do to our family.

And I'll never forget what those teachers and administrators did for our children during this difficult time in our family. Margaret, if somehow you are reading this book, we love you! I'm so grateful they had this opportunity to learn and grow in spite of everything.

POEMS FROM
THE KIDS

I have heard you can understand what's in a person's heart based on the poetry they write. So perhaps the best way to tell you how our kids felt about our time in Seattle is to hear it from their hearts. They wrote these as part of their extracurricular poetry class while attending Fred Hutch school. These were published in the book Based on a True Story: Just Beyond the Gate. Just imagine your kids reading these out loud to you…

My Poem Hides

My poem hides in my life experiences.

I think it's safe to say I love the wilderness.

Each and every day I think about my adventures to come,

I picture myself with Andrew, Curt and Jake having some fun.

My life is back at Coeur d'Alene.

Not in the city waiting for the brutal rain.

—Jordan, 16

Ode To Instability

I feel as if my body is barely holding it together

I spend each day and night trying to understand

What my purpose is, to see that beautiful Earth

I spend many hours wondering about what

Others think about me. I am barely hanging on.

I spend the rest of my day only wanting what I can't get. This crucial challenge

That I have been faced with will only get harder day by day until I figure out one

Important concept; God loves me for who I am.

—Jordan

Loneliness

Loneliness looks like the darkness, appears as the sun slips away

Into nothing but a memory. I feel as if the sun is taking advantage of me

As it shows itself only enough for me to depend on it.

Whether it be a day or a decade, I will soon figure out the breathtaking

Glow of the sun is surely undependable.

 —Jordan

Disappointment

Tastes like hot coffee, A never ending burn on your tongue.

Smells like medicine, striving to get rid of the feeling.

Sounds like a sad love song playing absent and alone in a chair.

Looking out at the city feels like a stab in the chest.

With no healing, looks like black with no stars to see above.

—Joya, 17

Haikus

When ocean meets sand

That's love, it kisses the shore

And comes back again.

The sound of your voice

Puts tears into my eyes and

Sends chills down my spine.

The cancer shall go

Farther away than the sun

Never coming back.

Words, they mean so much

I can't comprehend any

Brings you to the ground.

—Joya, 17

While we lived in Seattle, the two older kids, Joya and Jordan, took up running. They would take off together and run all over the city. My usually overprotective nature conceded to their sanity and I allowed them to go. They would come home out of breath, happier and telling stories about policemen who arrested a person while wrestling them to the ground to get their gun out of their hand. Strangely I didn't even have the mental or emotional energy to be worried at that time. Somehow I knew they would be okay, just like Chris would be okay. If it was raining hard, I would drop them off at the SCCA House, the other housing for cancer families, because they had a gym with treadmills.

All the kids struggled in their own ways. The little one, Jared, cried openly to me and talked about his feelings and fears of losing his dad. He spent the most time either visiting his dad in the hospital or snuggling with him in bed when he rested at home. Josh also vocalized his feelings openly but was far away at home, taking care of our house. He visited as often as he could. Joya cried a lot and asked me many times if her dad was going to die. I think she may have developed an eating disorder during this time. The psychologist on staff at the Hutch School let me know she was concerned. But I knew my daughter well enough to know she was going to make it through this.

Jordan really internalized it all. There were times when he was sitting on the patio of our 6th floor apartment, totally depressed, and I would pray that he wouldn't jump. One time after a running session on the treadmill alone, he came home and told me cried his eyes out while running that day. It really helped him feel better.

Not only was I worried about my husband's survival; I was worried about whether my kids were going to make it through in one piece. Usually the helicopter mom, I had to choose where to put my energy. I couldn't hover over the kids or worry about every little thing.

Once again, I put them securely in God's hands.

THE BAMBOO FARMER

I t was a foggy day in the Pacific Northwest, and Chris was feeling well enough that we enjoyed a walk to the nearest Starbucks. We hadn't been in Seattle very long and for now, all was holding steady. He was on the schedule for the many medical tests to begin in preparation for his transplant. It had been a couple of weeks since he had received any kind of chemo, either in his veins or his brain, so he actually felt pretty good.

Passersby sometimes did a double take at his looks. He was thin, pale and hairless and one of his eyes was drooping along with half of his face. He was wearing a white Nike T-shirt that said "Just Do It" on the front. As we walked into the entrance to the outside dining of the Starbucks, Mr Friendly, AKA Chris Harper, greeted a gentleman sitting at a table enjoying his beverage.

"How are you today?" Chris said. "Isn't it a beautiful day?"

If you didn't know him, based on his sunny disposition on this day, you would have thought he didn't have a care or problem in the world. My outlook was not nearly as sunny, and I wasn't the sick one! I was very worried about his transplant, and mulling things over constantly in my head, all while trying my best to remain positive and full of faith.

On our way out, this same man approached us.

"Are you familiar with the bamboo tree? he asked.

What a strange question.

"Bamboo? I guess," I said.

He handed us two little green rubber bracelets.

"Put these on," he said. The bracelets said WATER THE BAM-
BOO.

"Bamboo grows like no other plant in the world," the stranger
said. "But did you know? If you plant and water giant timber
bamboo, nothing visible happens the first year. Or again the second year. If you continue to water it for the third year not much
happens. But when you water it for the fourth year it will rocket
up an astonishing 90 feet in only 60 days!"

"That's incredible," Chris said. "Thank you."

Turns out the man was Greg Bell, a writer and speaker who
helps people look at the bright side of things. He'd been impressed with Chris's attitude. Greg is the author of *Water the
Bamboo, What's Going Well* and the *What's Going Well Companion
Journal.*

Once again, God had put something good in our path. Greg
and his bamboo story gave us one more little nugget to hang
on to. For the next several years, even when we didn't see much
progress in his recovery, we took great comfort in the bamboo
story. In fact, I even bought Chris a bamboo plant as a reminder.
Once again, we were deeply indebted to someone for their kind
words and deeds.

Even though it didn't look like Chris was improving on the
surface, we kept pressing on. We kept believing, knowing that
below the surface, his new blood cells were doing their thing.

All we had to do was look at that tiny, yet mighty bamboo
plant.

THAT SHOULD
HAVE KILLED YOU

"WHAT DOESN'T KILL YOU MAKES YOU STRONGER." —KELLY CLARKSON

W e had enjoyed the short window of calm before the storm, but it wasn't long before Chris's neurological symptoms started worsening again, this time in very odd ways.

Now he couldn't move his arm, in addition to his eye and side of his face. Then it switched sides! He had to use his hand to help his jaw move so he could chew his food.

They admitted him to the hospital to try to get him comfortable and run more tests, above and beyond the hundreds of tests being performed in preparation for his transplant. They tested his liver, his heart, his bones, his bone marrow, his brain. You name it, they tested it to make sure he was physically strong enough for the grueling procedure and to make sure he was truly in remission. They measured him for his radiation so they could protect his organs while they radiated the rest of his entire body, with special emphasis on his bone marrow, testicles and head.

His symptoms baffled his team of specialists. This meant a special visit to the neuro-oncologist along with more MRIs of his brain. The neuro-oncologist was shocked at the amounts of chemotherapy administered to Chris's in his brain. He showed us on the MRI that Chris had residual effects of this brain chemo and had some brain damage.

The neuro-oncologist actually told Chris he was lucky that the excess chemo in his brain didn't kill him. That being said, we always had total confidence in our local oncologist. For all we know it was his aggressive treatment that saved his life.

The only thing they could come up with was this brain damage was causing the strange neurological symptoms. And now, our Tan Team of specialists did not want to move forward with the transplant. They thought he was going to die anyway based on the worsening brain activity. If cancer was still present, why replace his marrow? Finally, his regular oncologist told them to go ahead. "Look, if he's going to die anyway then give him the transplant!" he essentially said. "At least give him a shot at living."

We are grateful for our doctor's advocacy, and also thankful we didn't hear about some of these statements until after the fact.

I was hugely relieved that we were moving forward. One of the first steps was inserting a more permanent central venous catheter, called a Hickman, to administer the pain medicines, the chemotherapy and eventually his food. This way they could also take blood anytime they needed for testing without having to stick him. He could even sleep through his blood draws now.

Even when he was able to eat in the normal way, the doctors warned Chris away from all his favorite foods. After all, he'd likely just be throwing it back up. Chris is a real foodie and was enjoying the delicious food Seattle had to offer that we couldn't get back home. He enjoyed having the kids over to his room so we could have dinner together.

One evening the doctor stopped by and found us all eating Thai food. The next night it was pizza, and Chris insisted on buying pizza for all his nurses. The doctor couldn't believe his eyes at the foods Chris was able to enjoy. Most of his transplant patients just could not eat like that during this phase of treatment.

I guess after a while, even chemotherapy becomes mundane, and you just go on living your life. Later on, when one of our friends ended up going to Seattle for the same lifesaving leukemia treatment, she asked the doctor if he knew Chris Harper. He thought about it for a moment and then said, "You mean the Thai food guy?"

This same doctor would sometimes come in his room on his morning rounds and check up on Chris. The doctor always seemed a little down. He would ask Chris how he was doing and Chris would always have the same answer. This was Chris the optimist, the patient the entire 7th floor of his home hospital came to know, remember? Now this unsuspecting doctor was about to get his reminder, too.

"Perfect" Chris would say and then ask the doctor, "How are you today?"

More often than not, the doctor would not answer the question to Chris's satisfaction.

"Oh I'm doing okay, I guess."

That didn't sit well with the cancer warrior strapped to a hospital bed while poison coursed through his veins. In Chris's mind, the doctor was on the other side of the bed, healthy as could be, with everything to live for. Chris enthusiastically corrected him.

"Well as far as I'm concerned you have a lot to be grateful for," Chris said. "So I'd say, you are perfect, too."

I have no idea what the doctor thought of that, but Chris had no tolerance for complainers or ungrateful people during his grueling cancer treatment. He still doesn't. Perhaps it was his background in the Marine Corp.

You don't get to complain when you're a Marine. Or if you're the Marine's wife or the Marine's kid.

THE PROPHECY
RETURNS

During Chris's hospital stay, pre-transplant, he insisted that I take the kids and go visit the prophetic pastor's home church in Seattle. So once again, the kids and I braved the hair-raising Seattle traffic and headed on a mission to go to a Tracey Armstrong church service. Chris asked me to make sure I spoke directly to Pastor Tracey. Actually, he insisted. Looking back, I think he was hoping the pastor prophet would tell me whether Chris was going to live or not.

No pressure or anything!

It meant so much to him, so how could I argue? And so the kids and I proceeded to sit through the world's longest church service. Jared's broken leg was still on the mend, so when the guest pastor called forward anyone who needed healing, I watched in amazement as my 12-year-old hopped out of his seat and limped, with his brace on, up to the stage for prayer.

The guest pastor was a very tall, thin, beautiful blonde woman. She looked like a model. After listening to some of her testimony and sermon, I found out that she was a fashion model. She prayed for our son and then as he walked back to his seat she called him out.

"Wait a second young man," she said. "God wants you to know you are a leader and you are called to be a leader to your friends at school and everyone."

She hit the nail on the head with this one. He is such a leader among his peers and wise beyond his years.

The service continued for several hours, and I'm not going to lie, my butt was hurting from sitting so long! What's that saying again? Your brain can only absorb what your ass can endure? Jordan finally decided to go and wait in the car, which I didn't blame him for. While he sat there, he witnessed a hit and run and became part of an investigation.

Toto, we're definitely not in Kansas anymore!

Meanwhile the service was ending. I searched the room for Pastor Tracey and found him surrounded by a couple of men who appeared to be bodyguards. I guess he was either very popular or else we were in a high crime area. The kids followed me as I stalked the minister. I basically had to run after him as he was leaving and the bodyguards weren't too happy with me chasing him. Nevertheless, Pastor Tracey saw me and let me approach.

"Do you remember me?" I asked. "You prophesied to my husband in Idaho. He got a leukemia diagnosis right afterwards."

"I do remember," he said. "And I'd heard that Chris had gotten sick. Whenever I thought of Chris, all I could picture was a pot of soil like one you would plant a flower in. I kept thinking of new growth. That thought would repeat itself over and over."

Amazing! He didn't know us, and probably barely remembered the prophecy. After all, he probably did that for hundreds of people.

"I have to tell you," I said. "My husband is about to receive a bone marrow transplant, wiping out his entire immune system and every single blood cell first. But I love your vision of the pot of soil. That image gives me comfort."

Why would he even think of Chris at all? Why would he picture a pot with fresh soil and think about new growth when thinking of him?

It reminded me of the chance encounter with Greg the bamboo man at Starbucks. With the second round of prophecy from Pastor Tracey, God sent me another little nugget of hope in the midst of an incredibly scary time.

Of course, I shared this with Chris the next day. I reminded him that new growth signaled his new blood cells taking off and good days were ahead of him. We chose to focus on that and thanked God for the new encounter and newfound faith. God is so good! On top of all that, the Lord also sent my youngest son away with new hope and a pep in his limpy step.

Sometimes our journey reminds me of the story in the bible about the woman with the issue of blood. She wasn't going to let anyone or anything hold her back from getting the healing she needed. That is how we were. Especially Chris. Our pride didn't stop us from going after any chance at healing that we had. Whether it was prayer, more prayer, seeking, worshipping God or having faith in his plan for Chris's life. As the story in Luke 8:43-48 goes:

"And a woman having an issue of blood twelve years, which had spent all her living upon physicians, neither could be healed of any, came behind him, and touched the border of his garment: and immediately her issue of blood stanched. And Jesus said, 'Who touched me?' When all denied, Peter and they that were with him said, 'Master, the multitude throng thee and press thee, and sayest thou, Who touched me?' And Jesus said, 'Somebody hath touched me: for I perceive that virtue is gone out of me.' And when the woman saw that she was not hid, she came trembling, and falling down before him, she declared unto him before all the people for what cause she had touched him, and how she was healed immediately. And he said unto her, 'Daughter, be of good comfort: thy faith hath made thee whole; go in peace.'"

That faith, that healing, that peace can be ours, too, my friends.

THE AUGUST 23RD MIRACLE

"A GRATEFUL HEART IS A MAGNET FOR MIRACLES."

T hese days, I always have to chuckle when someone says, "Here's my plan."

I used to be Exhibit A for a control freak, always making sure all my ducks were in a row. Looking back, it's hilarious. Leukemia, or life for that matter, doesn't obey orders.

Proverbs 16:9 says, "Within your heart you can make plans for your future, but the Lord chooses the steps you take to get there." *Amen to that!*

When the oncologist first told us the only path to a cure would be a bone marrow transplant, I asked him when this would take place. I wanted to plan everything, per usual. The doctor said it would be around October 2013, if everything went according to plan.

"When he gets the transplant, Chris will actually get a new birthday," the doctor said. "All of his old blood cells will be wiped out, yes, every last one, and every one of his blood cells will be brand new."

"Wouldn't it be so cool if he ended up with the transplant on my birthday, August 23," I said. "Then we could share a birthday."

The doctor laughed a little.

"Well, that's not really possible," he said.

I understood. It'd just been wishful thinking. By now I should have known that life and cancer never go as planned.

Now we were in Seattle and it was July 2013. And we were getting closer to transplant day. Chris was already admitted to the hospital because of all of the tests and his strange symptoms and I was telling Chris's nurse the birthday story.

"It looks like his transplant day will actually be August 22," she said.

"What a bummer," I said. " because I was so hoping we could share a birthday!"

She also laughed it off.

"It doesn't work that way," she said. "The blood products will arrive from Europe and immediately they have to be put into Chris's body."

The transplant was all set for August 22. We were down in the basement of the hospital in the radiation center waiting room. Chris had been there now for several days in a row, several times a day to get full body radiation. It was all part of the treatment to completely kill any cancer cells within his blood.

"I'm here for my sunbed visit," he would announce dramatically as they wheeled him in.

On top of the regular radiation, they literally had to put Chris's testicles on a platter while he laid still, his legs open to the radiation.

As I sat in the waiting room, their main hospital phone rang. I didn't think much of it.

"Is there a Shelley Harper in the room?" the front desk lady asked.

It caught me off guard, for sure. *Why would anyone be calling me here?*

I got on the phone and said, "Hello?" It was Chris's nurse Renee.

"I have some exciting news for you," she said. "The blood product from Europe has been delayed because of the donor."

Guess when Chris's new birthday would be? Yep, August 23!

So now we share a birthday! This little thing was such a big gift to me in our time of need; another nod from our Father in heaven. He knew how important this was to me.

I don't know why, I just thought it would be really cool. And God listened. Not only did He spare my husband, he did it in a very personal, mathematical sort of way. He is so good. Are you getting the picture? God loves us! He cares so deeply about the things that we care about that really don't even matter in the whole scheme of things. Call this a coincidence, but can you imagine the odds? I'm sure God had many more important things to do, but he did it anyway. This would be the best birthday gift I'd ever received.

The Bible says it well. Matthew 10:29-31 tells us, "Are not two sparrows sold for a copper coin? And not one of them falls to the ground apart from your Father's will. But the very hairs of your head are all numbered. Do not fear therefore; you are of more value than many sparrows."

If he has the hairs on your head numbered, then I can promise you He also knows your deepest desires.

The morning of Chris's lifesaving transplant was uneventful. We didn't know what exactly to expect other than someone else's bone marrow cells would be implanted into my husband so he could live. We also knew it would be his new birthday, so of course we had to have cake.

The kids and I arrived at the hospital around 3:30 a.m. because we didn't want to miss the exciting moment. We showed up with a cake that said *Happy Birthday Chris and Shelley*. We all had to gown up and put on our gloves to keep his room free from germs. Jordan had a bit of a scratchy throat so, as a precaution, he also wore a mask.

The nurse came in, hooked up the blood donation product and gave Chris what was essentially a blood transfusion. The whole process only took a couple of hours and was completely uneventful. The most exciting part of the whole procedure was eating the birthday cake at 4 a.m.

Of course we had to share our cake with those amazing

nurses, Renee, Kirk and Kara, who were taking such good care of my husband in his hour of need.

100 DAYS

"PEOPLE WHO ARE THE HAPPIEST IN LIFE DON'T HAVE THE BEST OF EVERYTHING, THEY MAKE THE BEST OF EVERYTHING THEY HAVE."

They warned us his white blood cells would be completely killed off. Zero cells left. I didn't really believe them. They weren't kidding. The next few mornings, as his blood was drawn to check all of the levels, there were NO white blood cells. This went on for about a week.

Did this thing work? I secretly wondered. I know Chris was wondering the same thing. We all were.

Meanwhile on the 8th floor of the hospital, the transplant floor, several code blues were announced and patients were lost. We know this because we saw all of the crying family members gathered in the waiting rooms. A code blue means an emergency situation and an urgent call for all medical personnel to try to resuscitate the patient.

Witnessing this was tough on morale. Just because Chris got the bone marrow transplant did not guarantee the successful outcome we were hoping for. We remained positive for the sake of our children, fully knowing that our hands were tied. But once again, where I should have had a pit in my stomach, I did not. I had peace. John 14:27 assures us, "I leave the gift of peace with you—my peace. Not the kind of fragile peace given by the world, but my perfect peace. Don't yield to fear or be troubled in your hearts—instead, be courageous!"

The way I understand this, it doesn't mean we won't feel fear at times, just that we won't *yield* to it.

But sure enough, about a week after the transplant, Chris had one white blood cell. Then the next day it was two. Then four. It kept doubling. It was working! There were some pretty gruesome side effects that he had to deal with, however. His mouth got a ton of sores. They were so severe he couldn't swallow or eat, a typical side effect of the chemotherapy and radiation. They used a suction tube for his saliva. In order to feed him, he was served liquid nutrition in his IV. It was called parenteral nutrition, a process in which all the required nutrients including protein, fat, calories, vitamins, and minerals was injected into his Hickman over the course of several hours.

He lost even more weight, a total of 50 pounds. He was living on opiate pain medicine to combat the pain of the mouth sores. As time wore on, he also developed a severe skin rash all over his face and body. I thought it was a side effect of the radiation, but we were told by the team of specialists that it was considered graft versus host disease, or GVHD. This is a complication of bone marrow transplants in which T cells in the donor bone marrow graft go on the offensive and attack the host's tissues. Most of the time it is seen in patients where the donor is unrelated to the patient. One way to offset this is to give the patient immune suppressing drugs. This doesn't always work though, and in Chris's case he got a pretty severe case on his skin and inside his mouth. Yet another battle for my wounded cancer warrior.

Once they decided Chris was out of the woods and could be discharged from the hospital, they still made sure we were living within ten minutes drive from Seattle Cancer Care Alliance center. He had daily appointments and they also wanted to be sure he was close in case of an emergency.

The SCCA clinic has a triage floor which is sort of like an urgent care or emergency room where you could bring the patient in the event of a fever or something unexpected. They were always checking his blood and temperature. That's where having the Hickman port implanted into his chest was so handy. They didn't have to re-poke him every time they needed to draw blood. This was especially nice when he was asleep. The nurses could come right in and grab his blood, most of the time without even waking him up. That sure beats a stick with a needle in the middle of a dream.

I always thought I wanted to be a nurse but after they discharged us I was starting to second guess that. I had to be the one to give Chris IV infusions of magnesium as well as fluids several times a day, and I did not feel qualified to be doing that. I also had to administer his medication. At one point I counted 37 pills that he had to take all at one time. They were constantly adjusting his medication. So just when I would finally feel like I had a handle on it, something would show up in his blood work and they would change things. I felt completely overwhelmed. Once again, I thought I might lose my mind, but somehow I kept going.

We had to constantly monitor for fever, which could be a very bad sign for a recovering bone marrow transplant patient. He didn't have much of an immune system so it was our job to keep all sickness away from him. The kids and I constantly washed our hands and used hand sanitizer. If we felt the slighted scratchy throat, we wore masks and avoided him. I just kept praying that God would keep me well since I was his caregiver. Somehow I did manage to stay healthy the whole time I was nursing him back to health.

I also tried my best to get him to eat and drink. He didn't have much of an appetite so I had to get creative. I felt like I had a toddler all over again. I would make deals with him.

"Okay, if you eat two bites of your pudding, we can watch what you want on TV."

Only I was making these deals with a grown man.

He was still on quite a bit of pain medication, so all he really wanted to do was sleep. He was forced to wake up to go to his doctor appointments and then back to bed he would go. His skin was peeling off from the radiation and the GVHD, and Jared would lie in bed with him and peel his shedding skin. To Jared it was a little game and frankly, gave him something to do to help his dad. When Chris got up to go to the bathroom, I would brush out the bed and vacuum the skin off of the floor really quick so he could get back in the bed.

Life went on. Our kids were still at Hutch School. I was still working from my laptop and doctor visits were still a daily part of our lives. Walking into the clinic, Chris looked like someone had dragged him behind a car. Chris would always talk to everyone in the elevator, because he's a friendly, outgoing guy.

Meanwhile, they would stare at him and his skin rash, not sure what to make of him. You could see their faces. Why was this guy with a strange skin disease talking to them? Was he contagious? But that didn't stop Chris.

"How are you today?" he would ask complete strangers. "Isn't it a beautiful day?"

Meanwhile, people stared at him like he had the plague. It always made me laugh that my husband had the best attitude of anyone in the place, healthy or not. And I have to believe that this positive attitude had something to do with his recovery.

Luckily, as time wore on he was able to be left with the boys for short periods so Joya and I could get away and maybe even do some window shopping. For us girls, buying groceries became our main source of fun and entertainment. There was a Starbucks inside the Safeway and I would always get a fancy drink and Joya would get a banana.

Good books were also a welcome distraction and a comfort to us during this time. Both Chris and I can recommend *Joy for Today*, a devotional book by Daryl Kraft which can be found on Amazon. This is about the Book of James, and is amazing for anyone going through a hard season. We both loved *Jesus Calling*, also found on Amazon. Both books encouraged us greatly. Whatever you are going through in life, big or small, I hope their message encourages you, too.

BUY THE DAMN PEPPERS!

IN HONOR OF THE BONASERA FAMILY AND THEIR BEAUTIFUL
DAUGHTER MICHELLE

Remember that day when Chris uttered what seemed to be the words of a crazy man? As the hospital staff frantically worked to save his life, he uttered these words:

"This is the best day of my life."

It sounds insane until you realize his mindset and his faith. Of course, he yearned to live and we yearned for him to live to defeat cancer, too. But whether God spared him or decided to take him home, Chris truly believed he couldn't lose.

It's an attitude and a faith that many people have remarked on and admired during his cancer journey. That faith shines through in a song that really spoke to me during our darkest hours. It still touches me deeply to this day.

We pray for blessings

We pray for peace

Comfort for family, protection while we sleep

We pray for healing, for prosperity

We pray for Your mighty hand to ease our suffering

All the while, You hear each spoken need

Yet love is way too much to give us lesser things

'Cause what if your blessings come through raindrops
What if Your healing comes through tears
What if a thousand sleepless nights are what it takes to know You're near
What if trials of this life are Your mercies in disguise

We pray for wisdom
Your voice to hear
We cry in anger when we cannot feel You near
We doubt your goodness, we doubt your love
As if every promise from Your Word is not enough
All the while, You hear each desperate plea
And long that we'd have faith to believe

When friends betray us
When darkness seems to win
We know that pain reminds this heart
That this is not our home

What if my greatest disappointments
Or the aching of this life
Is the revealing of a greater thirst this world can't satisfy
What if trials of this life
The rain, the storms, the hardest nights
Are your mercies in disguise?

Blessings —Laura Story

The Bible gives us the same hope in Corinthians 15:54-55, which says, "Death is swallowed up by a triumphant victory! So death, tell me, where is your victory? Tell me death, where is your sting?"

For a believer, death is not the end and we don't have to fear it. 1 Thessalonians 4:13-15 tells us, "Beloved brothers and sisters, we want you to be quite certain about the truth concerning those who have passed away, so that you won't be overwhelmed with grief like many people *who have no hope*. For if we believe that Jesus died and rose again, we also believe that God will bring with Jesus those who died while believing in Him. This is the word of the Lord: we who are alive in Him and remain on earth when the Lord appears will by no means have an advantage over those who have already died, for both will rise together."

And in Philippians 1:21, we read, "For to me, *to live is Christ*, and *to die is gain*."

It's Chris's win-win attitude. God is our source of joy, our reason to live. But if we pass away, we will be with Him in eternity.

These scriptures can be a powerful weapon against doubt and fear. As we see in Ephesians 6:13-18, "Therefore take up the whole armor of God, that you may be able to withstand in the evil day, and having done all, to stand firm. Stand therefore, having fastened on the belt of truth, and having put on the breastplate of righteousness, and, as shoes for your feet, having put on the readiness given by the gospel of peace. In all circumstances take up the shield of faith, with which you can extinguish all the flaming darts of the evil one; and take the helmet of salvation, and the sword of the Spirit, which is the word of God, praying at all times in the Spirit, with all prayer and supplication. To that end, keep alert with all perseverance, making supplication for all the saints."

My friends, when you are facing the struggle of your life, cancer or otherwise, use these precious scriptures as your armor. If living or dying is a win-win, what is left to attack? Of course, in human terms, the ones left behind suffer immensely, but still, we do not need to suffer as *those who have no hope!* In our case, we still get to enjoy our loved one. He's still with us, praise God!

But no one cheats death. We all experience this in the circle of life. We may as well live with hope and love and faith. This is a life well lived. Ultimately trusting God for the outcome.

I will never understand or be able to explain why some people beat cancer and others don't. That is not for me to understand. What I do understand is that God went before us. He prepped us in a sense for what we were going to face. He is with us. I know he has our back. I'm not afraid because no matter the challenge, I know He is with me and will never leave me.

One of my favorite scriptures is Psalm 139, 1-19, a wonderful passage that brings me great hope every time I read it. "Oh Lord, you have searched me thoroughly and have known me. You know when I sit down and when I rise up (my entire life, everything I do); You understand my thoughts from afar. You scrutinize my path and my lying down, and you are intimately acquainted with all my ways. Even before there is a word on my tongue (still unspoken), Behold O Lord, you know it all. You have enclosed me behind and before, and you have placed your hand upon me. Such infinite knowledge Is too wonderful for me. It is too high above me, I cannot reach it. Where can I go from your Spirit? Or where can I flee from your presence? If I ascend to heaven, you are there; If I make my bed in Sheol (the nether world, the place of the dead) behold, you are there. If I take the wings of the dawn, If I dwell in the remotest part of the sea, even there your hand will lead me, and your right hand will take hold of me. If I say, 'surely the darkness will cover me, and the night will be the only light around me.' Even the darkness is not dark to you and conceals nothing from you, but the night shines as bright as the day; darkness and light are alike to you. For you formed my innermost parts; you knit me together in my mother's womb. I will give thanks and praise to you , for I am fearfully and wonderfully made; wonderful are your works, and my soul knows it very well. My frame was not hidden from you, when I was being formed in secret, and intricately and skillfully formed (as if embroidered with many colors) in the depths of the earth. Your eyes have seen my unformed substance; *and in your book were all written the days that were appointed for me, when as yet there was not one of them* (even taking shape). How precious also are your thoughts to me, O God! How vast is the sum of them! If I could count them, they would outnumber the sand. When I awake, I am still with you. O that you would kill the wicked O God."

I've asked Chris sometimes, "How do you deal with losing your mom when you were just 17? Do you blame God or anything?"

His answer is always the same.

"I believe God has a book that contains our life, and all we need to do is turn the page," he says. "It's already written. So I never really blamed God when mom died. In fact, I learned firsthand that life is short, that we should make the most of every day."

I've always admired the way Chris truly lives and has taught me the same. *Make the memories. Have faith. Love fully. Trust God.*

We have a dear friend who suddenly lost her beautiful 19-year-old daughter Michelle in a car accident on her way back to college.

The mother will always cherish the last time they had dinner together. She was going to make Michelle's favorite meal, which was steak with peppers and onions. But at the grocery store, the peppers seemed too expensive.

So now it's her reminder of what's really important in life. She still tells us to this day, "Buy the damn peppers!"

We have taken this admonition to heart. As a family we live life in this manner and we always remind each other... *buy the damn peppers!*

MICHAEL BUBLE

"FOR A HAPPY LIFE, WANT WHAT YOU HAVE."

D uring our cancer journey, we encountered many kind-
nesses.

One was the people who donate tickets to Seattle
area events so cancer families can have a rare outing together.
Thanks to these gracious donations, we were able to go to the
Key Arena for a Women's National Basketball Association game.
Chris hadn't had chemo for a while, so his white blood counts
were high enough that he could be in public and exposed to normal germs.

As we were walking back to the car, I noticed the reader board
that listed all the performers who would be soon coming to the
Key Arena. One of them especially caught my eye. Michael Buble
would be performing there!

Being from a smaller city, we didn't often get these kinds of
opportunities. My heart longed to buy tickets and go to this
event, but my rational self immediately brushed this thought
away.

*I can't plan anything for tomorrow, much less a month from now.
And we can't afford frivolous spending on the concert tickets. It's just
a fantasy, a luxury item that doesn't fit our cancer budget or treatment timeline. Even with good health insurance, the medical bills are
piling up.*

So I tucked this thought deep away and drove the family back to our apartment, forgetting all about it.

Fast forward nearly four months. It was nearing Thanksgiving, and nearly at the end of Chris's treatment and his scheduled discharge date.

Then we had a really long day at the Seattle Cancer Care Alliance clinic. Chris had been complaining of rib pain. He assumed that he had pulled a muscle helping me unload some groceries, a luxury I had all but forgotten about. Since he had practically wasted away and lost 50 pounds, his strength way below normal. We now lived on the 6th floor of the Pete Gross House and per doctor's orders I encouraged him (Chris would say I yelled at him) to take the stairs rather than the elevator. He needed to rebuild his strength, since his major muscle groups including buttocks, thighs and so on had virtually wasted away from all of the prednisone use.

So with the new rib pain, he just assumed all this new activity was contributing to his new pain. Unfortunately that was not the case. That rib pain was a warning sign of what turned out to be eight separate embolisms in his lungs.

Pulmonary embolism is a blockage in one of the pulmonary arteries in your lungs. In most cases, it's caused by blood clots that travel to the lungs from the legs or, rarely, other parts of the body, called deep vein thrombosis. Because the clots block blood flow to the lungs, pulmonary embolism can be life-threatening.

Of course, Chris had to be exceptional. So he had, not just one, but eight of them. It was another reminder of how tough he was. With eight pulmonary embolisms, he had what he called "minor rib pain."

So that was what caused our long day at the outpatient clinic, getting treatment such as blood thinners and CT scans.

We were about to be discharged from the treatment and sent home to Idaho and we were concerned that this latest hurdle would negatively affect his release date. But the doctors didn't seem very concerned. I guess in the scheme of things, this was a minor setback. As we were leaving the clinic, I stopped at the front desk to grab a piece of candy and chat with the wonderful volunteers.

"How did the day go?" they asked.

"Well, it's honestly been a really long and mentally exhausting day," I had told them.

I explained Chris's medical setback, and said we'd also gotten a phone call from our kids' teacher letting us know that they had a rough day at school. One of the families represented at the Hutch School's father had passed away that day. He'd had a bone marrow transplant around the same time as Chris; however, his didn't work. Our kids had become friends with this family's children and were heartbroken for their family. It also stirred up some feelings of uncertainty in our own family's future since we were still not out of the woods.

One of the volunteers had been on the phone. She hung up and turned to me.

"So," she said. "Do you have any plans this evening?"

Hilarious, I thought.

"You mean, other than hanging out with my cancer patient?"

She laughed.

"Well, I just got off the phone and I have two tickets to the Micheal Buble concert tonight. They're yours if you want them."

I could barely contain my excitement.

Even as I write this, I can't help but giggle and tear up thinking about this remarkable coincidence.

I couldn't wait to tell Chris.

"Honey!" I said. "I have a last-minute chance to see Michael Buble tonight. They have two tickets and Joya and I could make it a girl's night out. The boys could stay with you. Would it be okay?"

I was practically begging. Chris could see how excited I really was.

"Of course, baby," he said. "You go enjoy that concert."

Under normal circumstances I don't think I would have left his side, but this was not normal circumstances.

It was Michael Buble!

We didn't have much time. I dropped Chris back off at the apartment with strict instructions for the boys what to look for.

"Your dad should do nothing but rest," I said. (not much different than the last nine months).

Off Joya and I went to the Key Arena to enjoy our much-needed girls' night out.

We found our tickets at will-call and made our way to our seats. We had to giggle because they were so high up in the arena that we would need binoculars to have seen him. We saw that some of our seatmates had indeed brought their binoculars along.

"Oh well," we said. "It's just amazing to be here."

A night out away from responsibility and cancer and baldness, and throwing up and crazy boys running around a small apartment.

We climbed back down the long sets of stairs to get a snack. Once we had our snacks and had started making our way back to our seats, a lady with a lanyard and name tag stopped us. She was young, pretty and very friendly.

"Could I see your tickets, please?" she said. "Do you have good seats?"

We girls giggled together.

"We're, uh, way up there!"

The nice lady grabbed our tickets and handed us a new pair.

"Not any more," she said with a big smile.

Joya and I looked down at the tickets. Our new seats were in the very front row.

We hugged each other, did our happy dance and profusely thanked this lady, yet another angel who had appeared in our lives.

Coincidence?

Maybe. But my heart will never forget how my Jesus blessed me with the biggest gift that day. It was more than the concert itself, which was amazing. Michael sang to *us* the entire night. It didn't even seem like anyone else was in the arena. But it was another reminder that God loved us. He hadn't forgotten about us, our well-being or any of that during this horrific journey.

It was as if He said, "I see you. I haven't forgotten about you. And I am with you."

Do you realize the chance of us getting those seats? Nearly impossible, I would imagine. I'd recently read a book by Mike Lindell, yes, the MyPillow guy, called *What Are the Odds?* He talked about how, despite the nearly non-existent chances, God had a hand in directing his life. For Joya and me, this was one of those moments.

As Micheal Buble was winding down his concert, he serenaded us with *Home*. As I heard those words, I finally broke down and cried, right there in the front row, in front of Michael and the world.

I'd been so strong, and Seattle had been so wonderful to us, but as soon as I heard those words, I knew I just wanted our family to go back home.

Another summer day

Has come and gone away

In Paris and Rome

But I wanna go home, mmm

May be surrounded by

A million people I

Still feel all alone

I wanna go home

Oh, I miss you, you know

And I've been keeping all the letters

That I wrote to you

Each one a line or two

I'm fine baby, how are you?

I would send them but I know
That it's just not enough
My words were cold and flat
And you deserve more than that

Another airplane
Another sunny place
I'm lucky I know
But I wanna go home
I've got to go home

Let me go home
I'm just too far
From where you are
I wanna come home

And I feel just like
I'm living someone else's life
It's like I just stepped outside
When everything was going right

And I know just why you could not
Come along with me
This was not your dream
But you always believed in me

Another winter day
Has come and gone away
In even Paris and Rome
And I wanna go home
Let me go home

And I'm surrounded by
A million people I
Still feel alone
And I wanna go home
Oh, I miss you, you know

Let me go home
I've had my run
Baby, I'm done
I'm coming home
Let me go home
It'll all be all right
I'll be home tonight
I'm coming back home

Home —Blake Shelton, Michael Bublé

HOME AGAIN!

"HOME... WHERE YOUR FEET MAY LEAVE... BUT NOT YOUR
HEART." —OLIVER WENDELL HOLMES

It was the day before Thanksgiving, and it was finally discharge day. We couldn't wait to have our final check up and
get out of Dodge. We met with one of our specialists named
Sasha and he told us goodbye.

"I knew you would make it," he said. "I always felt good vibes
coming from you."

He was brilliant and absolutely precious. So were Pat and
Joey, our nurses. It was bittersweet because our beloved Tan
Team had become more like family than medical professionals.

It was a dramatic moment as they took the Hickman device
out of Chris's chest, a parting medical procedure. We packed up
and drove out of the city limits and over the mountains, headed
east towards home.

As liberating as it was, it was also terribly scary, because now
Chris was solely in my care. He was still so weak that he could
barely walk a couple of blocks. He was recovering from his eight
pulmonary embolisms. His hands shook profusely like a 95-
year-old, side effects from medications he was on coupled with
his overall weakness. He still spent most of the day in bed.

But he was alive, we were an intact family unit, and we were
ready to pick up our Yorkie and be home for Thanksgiving. Our
friend "Grandma Diane" had graciously been dogsitting Oscar

for four months, free of charge.

I clearly hadn't had time to shop for groceries or even give Thanksgiving a second thought. We opened our front door and I lost it again and burst into tears.

There were fresh fruit and pies on the counter, along with notes and cards from some of our dear friends, and ready made Thanksgiving food in the fridge which only needed to be heated up.

How could we be so blessed to have such kind friends?

It was a difficult transition back into normal life. On one hand I was excited to get back to work, but on the other hand, that meant leaving Chris at home to fend for himself. His strength increased day-by-day, starting with walks to the mailbox and progressed to being able to work on a property we'd just bought. Cutting wood and cleaning up the place were like therapy to Chris, although it caused me a lot of angst.

He's not strong enough yet to be doing those things and using a chainsaw for God's sake! He's still rebuilding his immune system, and definitely not supposed to be digging in dirt or near fungus.

But of course, he's a hard-headed Marine! And by this point in our journey, I knew God held him in His hands.

Here's a typical day, post transplant. Doctor visit at 8:45 am, followed by a quick trip to the Safeway pharmacy down the street for a couple of immunizations. Not just any shots. These were baby booster shots, being administered to Chris, an adult. Because these aren't regular shots, the Safeway we went to didn't carry some of them. Even though I called two times ahead of time to make sure they were ready for us; when we got there, they didn't carry them. Along with that, they couldn't get the insurance to accept any of the charges, even though we had hit our deductible in the first or second month of the year with a $1,000,000 transplant.

So rather than paying $500 out of pocket and worrying about getting reimbursed later, we opted to pay for one of them (the one that other pharmacies were not likely to have) then head on down the road to a local Walgreens. I had also been in contact with this pharmacy, and was told they had everything in stock. Well, wouldn't you know it. They didn't. So Chris got what shots he could, then we had to order one for a later date.

They also could only get some of the shots to go through the insurance, while others we had to pay for up front. More than $160 later, we were out the door. By now it was 2 p.m. and I had a full day's worth of work to get done by 5 p.m.

We'd been told they won't even let you get a bone marrow transplant unless you have a full-time caregiver, and now I understand why. And caregiver is not an easy role. You definitely have a chance to work on your patience, because things and appointments take forever and there's absolutely nothing you can do about it. You're at everyone else's mercy. I thanked God every single day that my job was so flexible. At the same time, I had to be extra efficient. I needed to get the same amount of work done as the next guy, but usually in half the time.

Even when I was at work, my mind was on my husband, wondering if he had eaten, taken his pills, or if he was doing something that physically he should not be attempting.

Did he remember to turn the stove off this time?

If I had a dollar for every minute I've spent waiting on a doctor, a test result, an insurance company or in a pharmacy line I would be a millionaire by now.

But of course, I would do it a million times over, just to have my Chris still by my side.

ONE-AND-A-HALF YEARS AFTER

"PATIENCE IS NOT PASSIVE. ON THE CONTRARY, IT IS CONCEN-
TRATED STRENGTH." —BRUCE LEE

I t was time for Chris's monthly lab work and office visit with his oncologist.

His dosage of immunosuppressant medication had recently increased. So now they wanted to check his blood levels on a regular basis to guard against the spread of cytomegalovirus. This sinister-sounding virus is common in many people, and once infected, your body has CMV for life. When you're healthy, it's not a problem. But with Chris taking all his immunosuppressants, CMV could kill him.

"I've got a question for you," I asked the doctor. "Something else that's been worrying me. We met another doctor whose wife had leukemia and a bone marrow transplant. That was six years ago, and now she has GVHD so bad that she's at only 40 percent lung capacity. My understanding is that she will never get better. Her life now has huge limitations. She's on oxygen and can hardly walk. She can no longer do fun things with her husband and kids. To tell you the truth, we personally know several horrible cases of GVHD, of the stomach, kidneys, joints, skin, eyes and mouth."

"Yes, it's impossible to predict what will happen with GVHD," the doctor said.

"And I guess one of the reasons it happened was she got off of her immune suppressant drugs too soon, at her physician's recommendation. Once she did this, the GVHD spread to her lungs so quickly and got out of hand so fast that the damage was already done before anyone had a chance to react. I've got to tell you, it left both Chris and I downright depressed and a little freaked out about it. I mean, this lady was a marathon runner and now look at her!"

"Well, I have some reassurances for you," our doctor said. "You cannot compare apples to oranges. Their disease was different. Yes, GVHD is always a possibility, But In the meantime, I want to remind you how fortunate we are that Chris is healthy, that he beat leukemia, that in one more year we can rest a little easier that his leukemia will never be back."

It was good to hear this encouragement from one of our heroes on our cancer journey. This man helped save my husband's life and we will forever be grateful.

Our son Jordan had just become a Marine. What an amazing thing for Chris, the former Marine, to proudly see his son take up the cause, to watch him graduate Marine Corps boot camp with all the patriotic festivities. Chalk it up to yet another precious memory that my husband got to be a part of. We will *never* take any of these memories for granted.

So after the doctor's appointment, we went with Jordan, our new Marine, to the Dealer's Auto Auction. And at that event I watched something light up inside Chris. I saw that spark of energy and excitement in him as each of the auction cars drove up.

Something clicked. I heard the words of Pastor Tracey's prophecy. *You are an entrepreneur. That's your calling. You're going to feed nations and build churches. That's inside of you. You want to be able to do that.*

I looked over at Chris and said, "This is your time. The day is finally here. You've been wanting to help the boys start their business. Do it!"

Chris looked back at me and gave me that grin. I got a thrill down to my toes, knowing my man was back in the game, doing what he loved to do again.

Josh and Jared had attempted to start a motorsports rental business but they needed help and dad's expertise and a dealer license. Chris was still debating whether or not he had the energy to jump in. And this was four years after his transplant! It took that long to heal.

It never ceases to amaze me how the words the prophet spoke over my husband and family still continue to ring true. I used to think that God would hit us over the head. We would see a burning bush speaking to us saying, "do this ministry, or go over there to preach the gospel."

But instead we heard the still, small voice. We were called to be the salt of the earth in Matthew 5:13: "You are the salt of the earth; but if the salt loses its flavor, how shall it be seasoned? It is then good for nothing but to be thrown out and trampled underfoot by man."

But through our cancer journey, I've also learned that, in order to be salt, you have to go through things. You are not born ready to be salt. You can't help season someone else until you have flavor yourself. Until you have something to offer. You can't share hope or faith or love or forgiveness until you've lost, you've fought, you've struggled and hurt yourself and others.

Those who have felt the deepest hurt can share the greatest help. Now they can be the light in a dark world. In our daily lives, in school, at our jobs, in our professions, in the military, we are all called to be the salt, to give the world flavor.

And only in this daily walk of life can we truly share the things God has done.

When you've been to the cancer ward, you know the truth. You can walk right up to a newly diagnosed cancer patient and their family. You can look them squarely in the eye.

You can say, "There is HOPE."

And you will mean it with all your heart.

NEW BLOOD

"AT THE END OF THE DAY, ALL THAT MATTERS IS LOVE AND MEMORIES, SO MAKE SURE YOU GIVE IT AND MAKE SURE YOU MAKE THEM." —TRENT SHELTON

As I give gratitude to God for his many blessings, I have to include all the beautiful memories.

I think of how many things Chris has been able to experience since his diagnosis. He dared to dream, and now he has lived those dreams.

He saw his daughter Joya graduate high school and celebrate with family and friends. He also saw his sons Jordan and Jared graduate. He even served as the master BBQ chef at their graduation parties. He was there when his son Jordan became a United States Marine. He has had many amazing vacations in fabulous places since his cancer journey.

Fishing for tarpon with his boys in Belize, hunting elk by hiking up and down mountains more than 15 miles a day, taking me to Europe for a romantic three-week trip. This was after wondering if he'd ever be strong enough to hunt again or if he could travel without fears of getting pneumonia.

Most important of all, he is now a grandpa to two bouncing bundles. He has walked his daughter down the aisle and officiated his own son Josh's wedding.

At his darkest moments, Chris dared to dream.

And since you are reading his story, I want you to know that you can dare to dream, too. I want you to know that you can beat what you are battling, whatever it is.

"You've got this," Chris the eternal optimist would tell you.

Jeremiah 29:11 says, "For I know the plans and thoughts that I have for you, says the Lord, plans for peace and well-being and not for disaster, to give you a future and a hope."

And I also want you to know something amazing. If you are reading this and there's a chance your battle might kill you, then please know there is also cause for great hope; the hope of eternity spent with the Lord. There is no greater destination than eternity with the one who created you. We should all aspire to this great truth, since we all will face him one day.

You could repeat this prayer, "Dear Jesus, I ask that you would be the Lord of my life. Forgive my sins and comfort me and be with me all of my days."

It's so very simple, but so profound, this gift that Jesus offers. People and religion often overcomplicate things, but my cancer warrior husband has a wonderfully simple way of explaining it.

"I now have the blood of another man in my body," Chris says. "It's his new blood for me. I'm no longer even the same old blood type. It was Type A and now I'm Type O. Jesus did the same swap for us. He shed his blood on a cross, he was God and man, and because of this he died to wipe out the sins of the world."

John 3:16 says, "For God so greatly loved and dearly prized the world, that He even gave His one and only begotten Son, so that whoever believes and trusts in Him (as Savior) shall not perish, but have eternal life."

And that, my friends, is the greatest hope of all. We are all going to die someday and only God knows how and when. Why not go through life with hope? Hope while you are living that God is directing your steps and is always one step ahead of you. Hope in death, knowing you will be with him. That is the ultimate WIN-WIN.

Jesus did that swap for you and me. He took our old nature and our sins, and transfused into us His new shed blood so we can stand pure before Him. Just like Chris's donor gave his blood out of the kindness of his heart so Chris could live, Jesus gave his blood on a cross, enduring an awful death so we can live eternally.

It's the ultimate gift. Nothing Chris could do could repay his donor for his kindness, just like nothing you and I could do could possibly repay God for the sacrifice of Jesus.

So how does Chris repay his donor? To live each minute as if it were his last! To pay the kindness forward. To live with faith and hope and love. And to see each and every sunrise as a precious, precious gift.

I CAN ONLY IMAGINE

"WILL I DANCE FOR YOU JESUS, OR IN AWE OF YOU BE STILL?"

There was one song that helped us through our cancer journey more than any other.

I Can Only Imagine.

When Chris was hurting the most, he would ask me to play this song. It would take his mind to a sacred place, as if he and God were the only ones in the room. Tears would run down his cheeks.

It became such an important song to him that I couldn't bear to hear it alone. If it came on the radio when I was by myself, I would change the station. It made me sad. It reminded me that I would not have Chris forever, that he is just a gift from God for a period of time on this earth.

The movie, *I Can Only Imagine,* is an amazing story of forgiveness and hope, but to this day I can barely get through it and I always cry. Every time I hear this beautiful song today, it brings back so many memories.

I can only imagine

What it will be like

When I walk by your side

I can only imagine

What my eyes would see

When your face is before me

I can only imagine

I can only imagine, yeah

Surrounded by your glory

What will my heart feel

Will I dance for you Jesus

Or in awe of You be still

Will I stand in your presence

To my knees will I fall

Will I sing hallelujah

Will I be able to speak at all

I can only imagine

I can only imagine

I can only imagine

When that day comes

And I find myself

Standing in the sun

I can only imagine

When all I will do

Is forever, forever worship you

I can only imagine

I can only imagine

Surrounded by your glory

What will my heart feel

Will I dance for you Jesus

Or in awe of You be still

Will I stand in your presence

Or to my knees will I fall

Will I sing hallelujah

Will I be able to speak at all

I can only imagine, yeah

I can only imagine

Surrounded by your glory

What will my heart feel

Will I dance for you Jesus

Or in awe of You be still

Will I stand in your presence

Or to my knees will I fall

Will I sing hallelujah

Will I be able to speak at all

I can only imagine yeah

I can only imagine yeah yeah

I can only imagine yeah yeah

I can only imagine

I can only imagine yeah yeah

I can only imagine

I can only imagine

When all I will do

Is forever, forever worship you

I can only imagine.

I Can Only Imagine —Bart Millard, Mercy Me

WE THOUGHT YOU WERE TOAST

"COURAGE DOESN'T ALWAYS ROAR. SOMETIMES IT'S THE QUIET VOICE AT THE END OF THE DAY WHISPERING, I WILL TRY AGAIN TOMORROW." —MARY ANNE RADMACHER

"**W**ow, it's you guys! Amazing to see you again."

It was our Tan Team nurse, Pat. We were back in Seattle for a checkup.

Pat gave us both a big hug.

"I can't believe how good you look," she told Chris. "I didn't even know if you'd survived."

"Happy to be here," Chris said.

"I have to confide something," Pat said. "When you first came in here, you were so sick. Some of the staff here thought you were toast."

Thank you for God's grace. And thank you that we didn't hear that earlier.

Chris made it through his checkups in Seattle with flying colors, but back home we ran into another rather scary complication.

He got a cough, which became worse and eventually sounded like he had metal in his chest. Back we went to his faithful oncologist, who by now was like another member of our family. I remember Chris was coughing so loudly and frequently that he basically cleared out an entire waiting room of immuno-compromised cancer patients. But we had nowhere else to turn, since a regular emergency room isn't equipped to treat a bone marrow transplant patient.

The cough became severe pneumonia, and Chris was admitted to our local hospital. When you love someone who had leukemia and who survived by getting a bone marrow transplant, pneumonia is always in the back of your mind.

Like a lot of other things in life, it's just as well you don't know the whole story when you move forward with the transplant. So many transplant patients survive only to be wiped out by a complication down the road. Pneumonia is one of the biggies. That's what killed the other Chris Harper when we saw his obituary in the paper. The body is in a weakened state after undergoing a bone marrow transplant and the patient's immune system is virtually nonexistent, more like that of a newborn. All of a person's previous immunities to viruses and diseases are gone and they take time to come back.

The tiniest of viruses can be a very big deal. So for a lifelong worrywart like me, you can imagine the overwhelming fears associated with, not only a leukemia diagnosis, but then the treatments and risks involved. I'm not sure what's worse on the fear scale, leukemia or the risks from treatment for leukemia. To survive seems to be the biggest risk of all!

After all the time we'd spent in a hospital room, our week back in the hospital felt a little like going home. Thankfully, Chris overcame the bug. But he told me afterwards he was actually more scared during this than even the cancer ordeal. He wasn't sure if he would pull through.

After this we became quite vigilant. At the first sign of a cough, or if we were planning any kind of travel, our doctor would prescribe either antivirals or antibiotics. This plan of attack seemed to work. You can imagine the challenge of trying to keep your loved one away from germs, dirt, fungus and sick people. Never take your health for granted! If you have a working immune system, be so grateful for that. It's a nightmare when you don't.

For several years after the transplant, I was hypersensitive to say the least about any sick people near my husband. When we would go to church or another public place, God forbid anyone would cough near us (and this was pre-COVID-19) because we would clear out. Eventually Chris's immune system became strong again. He has traveled around the world and been able to stay healthy, just like anyone else.

What a blessing!

Long before COVID-19 I was known as the hand sanitizer Nazi. If any of our kids' friends came over, the first thing they did was wash their hands, because they knew the entire situation.

"Have you gotten your flu shot?" I would ask. If not, I wouldn't let them come over until they did.

Those kids were so awesome. Not just ours, but their friends too. They all did everything they could to help Chris get well and stay well. They all loved him.

A funny thing happened while Chris was hospitalized with pneumonia. While I was there visiting him, one of my migraines came on, along with extreme nausea.

So there I was, in his hospital room, throwing up in his hospital toilet, while my sweet, sick husband held my hair out of the way and rubbed my back to comfort me.

And who should walk in right? Our pastors, J.O. and Raydeane.

Talk about another humorous yet humbling experience. We seemed to be making a habit of both.

Raydeane Owens knows about wisdom and strength. She's written an inspiring book about her journey called Heaven/Earth, available on Amazon. In her book, she says,

"Difficult seasons were never meant to break us, but to make us. We discover so much of our core identity when we are faced with challenges. None of us want to do the work involved in remaking unless we are pressed. The way we face our shadow days allows us to gratefully embrace our days in the sun."

Amen to that.

A CHURCH IN INDIA

"LET GENEROSITY BE THE BOSS OF ME." —PASTOR J.O.

One after another, amazing things continued to come out of our cancer story.

During Chris's recovery period after his transplant, we found ourselves extra connected to God, to church and to what was truly important in life. And evidently our children were, too.

Our family went to a church service where they had a guest speaker from India, and the pastor described how $10,000 would give the community in India a church, a school house and a place for fresh water, all in one.

Chris was giving Jared a ride to school the next morning when Jared, out of the blue, made an announcement.

"By the time I graduate high school I want to build one of those churches," he said.

Chris came home and immediately told me the story with tears in his eyes.

"You know what?" he said. "As far as I'm concerned, I've arrived. This might just be the proudest moment of my life. To know that we've raised generous and loving kids. That is a true legacy."

Remember that, prior to the prophecy and his cancer diagnosis, Chris had been desperately asking God to give him a legacy. And here it was!

Knowing our kids, this wish had a very good chance of becoming reality. And it did. By the time he was 16 years old, Jared had in fact saved up the $10,000. An impressive feat, considering he was a high school kid and made the money from flipping cars and motorcycles, somehow finding time along with sports and his other responsibilities. His brothers and sister also chipped in to help. And just like he promised, Jared was able to mail off a check to that pastor in India.

I don't want to sound like I'm bragging about my boy (well, maybe just a little bit). I also want to respect his reasons for his quietly generous gift. "When you give, give in secret," as Matthew 6 says. I know the truth. It had everything to do with his heart and nothing to do with his ego.

But this is a story worth passing along. I hope it inspires hope that really, really, really good things will come out of a terrible situation, if we only let go and let God work.

And isn't it wonderful to know that Chris's heartfelt plea to God for a legacy would be so lovingly rewarded? That he was spared and still alive to see his legacy in action?

Even from the depths of our despair, and especially then, God hears our cry.

THE HOLY SPIRIT IS MY BEST FRIEND

"YOU CARRY MY WEAKNESS, MY SICKNESS, MY BROKENNESS
ALL ON YOUR SHOULDERS." —FOR KING & COUNTRY

S ince the time I can remember, the Holy Spirit has been my best and closest friend. It's why I dearly love the beautiful depiction in the 23rd Psalm.

The Good Shepherd: David's poetic praise to God

The Lord is my best friend and my shepherd.

I always have more than enough.

He offers a resting place for me in his luxurious love.

His tracks take me to an oasis of peace, the quiet brook of bliss.

That's where he restores and revives my life.

He opens before me pathways to God's pleasure

and leads me along in his footsteps of righteousness

so that I can bring honor to his name.

Lord, even when your path takes me through

the valley of deepest darkness,

fear will never conquer me, for you already have!

You remain close to me and lead me through it all the way.

Your authority is my strength and my peace.

The comfort of your love takes away my fear.

I'll never be lonely, for you are near.

You become my delicious feast

even when my enemies dare to fight.

You anoint me with the fragrance of your Holy Spirit;

you give me all I can drink of you until my heart overflows.

So why would I fear the future?

For your goodness and love pursue me all the days of my life.

Then afterward, when my life is through,

I'll return to your glorious presence to be forever with you!

—Psalm 23 The Passion Translation (TPT)

I'm also going to share with you a wonderful song that got me through my most chaotic times. I encourage you to really pay attention to these words.

I look up to the mountains

Does my strength come from the mountains?

No, my strength comes from God

Who made heaven, and earth, and the mountains

When confusion's my companion

And despair holds me for ransom

I will feel no fear

I know that You are near

When I'm caught deep in the valley

With chaos for my company

I'll find my comfort here

'Cause I know that You are near

My help comes from You

You're right here, pulling me through

You carry my weakness, my sickness, my brokenness all on Your shoulders

Your shoulders

My help comes from You

You are my rest, my rescue

I don't have to see to believe that You're lifting me up on Your shoulders

Your shoulders

You mend what once was shattered

And You turn my tears to laughter

Your forgiveness is my fortress

Oh Your mercy is relentless

My help comes from You

You're right here, pulling me through

You carry my weakness, my sickness, my brokenness all on Your shoulders

Your shoulders

My help comes from You

You are my rest, my rescue

I don't have to see to believe that You're lifting me up on Your shoulders

Your shoulders

My help is from You

Don't have to see it to believe it

My help is from you

Don't have to see it, 'cause I know, 'cause I know it's true

My help is from You

Don't have to see it to believe it

My help is from you

Don't have to see it, 'cause I know, 'cause I know it's true

My help comes from You

You're right here, pulling me through

You carry my weakness, my sickness, my brokenness all on Your shoulders

Your shoulders

My help comes from You

You are my rest, my rescue

I don't have to see to believe that You're lifting me up on Your shoulders

Your shoulders

My help is from You

Don't have to see it to believe it

My help is from you

Don't have to see it, 'cause I know, 'cause I know it's true

Shoulders —For King & Country

May God bless David for writing the Psalms. And may He bless the singers and songwriters of our gospel music of today for letting my beloved Holy Spirit shine through their work, and sharing their comfort with us all.

HOLD MY GRANDBABIES FOR ME!

"PRECIOUS IN THE SIGHT OF THE LORD IS THE DEATH OF HIS
SAINTS." —PSALM 116:15

C hris was now gaining endurance day by day. We were raising our kids and doing life together.

Jared's baseball games were very much a part of that life. One of our favorite baseball coaches was a young man named Colby who was around Joya's age. I loved how he interacted with the kids. He seemed shy around us parents, but was a playful and fun coach to the boys.

Not long after the season started, we found out that his beautiful mom Tammi had been diagnosed with leukemia at age 45, just like Chris. This ripped our hearts out because we knew what his family was going through. We brought them dinner and introduced ourselves to the family. We let them know if they needed anything or had any questions about the treatments, they could call us anytime.

Her treatment also went well, and she, too, had to get a bone marrow transplant. She went to Seattle, had all of her treatments and came back home to finish her recovery.

As our families got to know each other, our daughter and

Jared's coach Colby became close and started dating. How crazy it was that both the kids had a parent who had or was battling leukemia! What are the odds?

Here's a funny aside. When Colby found out Jared was Joya's brother, he'd pestered him for details.

"Does she ever talk about me?" he'd asked.

Jared replied like a typical little brother.

"Nope," he said. "She's never even mentioned your name."

What a little stinker!

We celebrated Colby's 21st birthday with his mama and she was so happy to be there. She was pretty sick that day, though, and it concerned us. Not long after that, she was able to witness her son getting baptized in beautiful Lake Coeur d'Alene. I know this was a high point of her life. She was beaming with pride, even though she didn't feel very good and had little energy. She wasn't really thriving and improving like I had expected; but Chris's recovery had taken a really long time, too, so we kept on being patient.

Sadly, not long after her son's baptism, Tammi's health really took a turn for the worse. We visited her in the hospital and prayed for her. Before we knew it, she was transported back to Seattle for further treatment. Because transplant patients have a lot of setbacks during their recovery, I wasn't overly alarmed. But soon she was on her deathbed.

Surrounded by her family, she reached out and gripped her own mother's hand.

"Please, hold my grandbabies for me," she whispered. Not long after, she took her last breath on Earth.

I think of Tammi every day. She was such a precious woman and I know she is celebrating with God. Even if she had the chance to be back on Earth she wouldn't take it, because she is at peace.

I tell her story because she served the same God Chris serves. She virtually had the same disease and the same treatment. We prayed for her, too. Now she is with Jesus. She received the healing we prayed for, just in a different way.

There are just so many things that we don't understand on this earth but her story reminds me to live each day as a gift. To be sure to appreciate my loved ones, even if they do something to annoy me. She was a precious woman and now she has a darling grandbaby named Reese Tammi in her honor. She also has an eternal legacy that will live forever.

Whenever I'm with that sweet baby, the child her precious son and our beautiful daughter made, I talk to Tammi.

I always let her know I'm holding her grandbaby for her.

THIS IS HOW WE FIGHT OUR BATTLES

"THIS AIN'T FOR EVERYBODY, TOES HANGING OFF THE LEDGE
LIKE WE GOT NOTHIN' TO LOSE; AIN'T ALWAYS HEAVEN, BABY,
THIS LIVIN' ON THE EDGE; YOU HOLDIN' ME, HOLDIN' YOU, IT'S
A HELL OF A VIEW." —ERIC CHURCH

There are many days where the cancer journey truly feels like a never-ending battle. On days like that, Chris and I love to turn up the volume on this song.

The Word says

"For the spirit of heaviness

Put on the garment of praise"

That's how we fight our battles

This is how I fight my battles

This is how I fight my battles

This is how I fight my battles

This is how I fight my battles

It may look like I'm surrounded but I'm surrounded by You

It may look like I'm surrounded but I'm surrounded by You

It may look like I'm surrounded but I'm surrounded by You

It may look like I'm surrounded but I'm surrounded by You...

This is how we fight

This is how we fight our battles

This is how we fight our battles

This is how we fight our battles

Surrounded (Fight My Battles) —Michael W. Smith

As a believer, how are we supposed to fight our battles? By praising God!

But that makes no sense, you say.

Perhaps not, but that is the choice our family made. We chose to praise and worship during the darkest times. Not for what we could get out of it, but because it made a difference in how we were able to cope. Praise lifted our spirits and brought our hopes alive again. We had peace as we sang or listened to the worship music we chose to surround ourselves with. still do.

Even now, the first thing Chris does in the morning is put on a worship song. He closes his eyes and he goes somewhere. A place of utter peace.

Does that mean that we didn't have our huge failures? Oh my gosh, no! We had our epic fights. There was that time Chris was on high doses of steroids and didn't like my Seattle driving and told me to pull over he was going to walk the rest of the way. I was happy to oblige. Luckily we were nearly to the clinic door by then.

Or the time we were walking through Seattle to regain his strength, and he insisted on walking IN the street rather than on the sidewalk, while almost getting himself killed a couple of times. You bet there was a fight that day.

And don't even get me started on the day he ran away and we

searched for him all over town.

But God in his beautiful mercy took our ashes, and I promise you he has turned them into a thing of beauty, just like Isaiah 61 promises. I love that about God. He doesn't expect us to be perfect. He loves us in the exact shape, place and mood we are in right now. He loves our scars. In fact, He shares our scars. Some of those scars we can see and some are invisible to everyone but our Lord. Those scars are simply proof that we are victorious.

It's okay to be a broken mess right now. It's okay to be scared out of your mind because you just got some devastating news. It's okay not to have all the answers. God sees you. He is with you right now. Reach out to him. He wants to be with you. He can handle the truth, so talk to him. He already knows what you are thinking anyway.

The real question is, how will you choose to fight your battles today?

GRATITUDE, THE ONLY REAL CURRENCY

"THERE IS ALWAYS, ALWAYS, ALWAYS SOMETHING TO BE
THANKFUL FOR."

Gratitude is the single biggest thing that has changed my life. It's so cliché, but life really is what you make it. Are you watching for the silver lining? It's there, if you look hard enough. I promise. I know it's easier said than done. I've struggled with it at times in my life.

Wait a minute! At times? Who am I kidding? I struggle with this every day!

To be sure, our natural temperament and brain chemistry plays a role. Some people wake up with a smile on their faces and everything that happens to them is spectacular. That would be my husband. Others can hardly drag themselves out of bed and feel like they are carrying a lead balloon around. And that would be me.

It takes work to cultivate this attitude of gratitude, this *What's going well?* mindset.

Perhaps today I'm in a lot of pain from my chronic back injury. It would be very easy for me to curl up into a little ball in tears and stay there. Yes, I did that last week.

Or, I can dig deep and look for *just one thing* I'm grateful for. Sometimes one thing is all you can come up with. That one thing may be the fact that you are breathing air in and out of your lungs. That may be it. Then focus on your breath. Thank God for it. Thank him again. And again. And again. Think about how fortunate you are that you can get breath into and out of your lungs.

Can you walk a block? Some people cannot. This is something we take for granted. Do you have a pet? Be thankful for that animal in your life. Some days we can just sit there and rub our pets and be thankful for them. Are you sitting in a hospital right now? Be grateful that you can be at a hospital! We live in a country where we have access to excellent medical care. Focus on how grateful you are to have that option. Do you have a person in your life you can call on? A spouse? A child? A mom, dad or brother? How about an in-law? Do you have one single friend? Then you are blessed. Be grateful for them!

I return to that wonderful advice in Philippians 4, "...offering your faith-filled requests before God with overflowing gratitude...God's wonderful peace that transcends human understanding will make the answers known to you through Jesus Christ."

In 1 Thessalonians 5:16-18, we read, "Let joy be your continual feast. Make your life a prayer. *And in the midst of everything be always giving thanks*, for this is God's perfect plan for you in Christ Jesus."

As the saying goes, "It's not happiness that brings us gratitude, it's gratitude that brings us happiness."

I promise you if you practice finding gratitude you will transform your life. I recommend a great book called *The Gratitude Jar: A Simple Guide to Creating Miracles* by Josie Robinson.

"Gratitude unlocks the fullness of life. It turns what we have into enough, and more. It turns denial into acceptance, chaos to order, confusion to clarity. It can turn a meal into a feast, a house into a home, a stranger into a friend." —Melody Beattie

Every morning now, as soon as he wakes up, Chris makes it a

habit to thank God that he gets another day. And now his habit is my habit.

I encourage you to make that a habit, too.

Today, and every day, nearly 150,000 people worldwide will die of various causes. They will not have that chance.

Have you stopped to thank God for giving you another day?

ANOTHER IN THE FIRE

"THERE IS A GRAVE THAT HOLDS NO BODY, AND NOW THAT POWER LIVES IN ME."

I want to share another comforting song. It reminds us that we might go through hard times, but never alone.

There's a grace when the heart is under fire

Another way when the walls are closing in

And when I look at the space between

Where I used to be and this reckoning

I know I will never be alone

There was another in the fire

Standing next to me

There was another in the waters

Holding back the seas

And should I ever need reminding

Of how I've been set free

There is a cross that bears the burden

Where another died for me

There is another in the fire

All my debt left for dead beneath the waters

I'm no longer a slave to my sin anymore

And should I fall in the space between

What remains of me and this reckoning

Either way I won't bow to the things of this world

And I know I will never be alone

There is another in the fire

Standing next to me

There is another in the waters

Holding back the seas

And should I ever need reminding

What power set me free

There is a grave that holds no body

And now that power lives in me

There is another in the fire, oh

There is another in the fire, whoa

There is another in the fire, whoa

There is another in the fire, oh

I can see

And I can see the light in the darkness

As the darkness bows to Him

I can hear the roar in the heavens

As the space between wears thin

I can feel the ground shake beneath us

As the prison walls cave in

Nothing stands between us

Nothing stands between us

There is no other name but the name that is Jesus

He who was and still is, and will be through it all

So come what may in the space between

All the things unseen and this reckoning

And I know I will never be alone

And I know I will never be alone

There'll be another in the fire

Standing next to me

There'll be another in the waters

Holding back the seas

And should I ever need reminding

How good You've been to me

I'll count the joy come every battle

'Cause I know that's where You'll be

I can see the light

And I can see the light in the darkness

As the darkness bows to Him

I can hear the roar in the heavens

As the space between wears thin

I can feel the ground shake beneath us

As the prison walls cave in

Nothing stands between us

Nothing stands between

There'll be another in the fire

Standing next to me

There'll be another in the waters

Holding back the seas

And should I ever need reminding

How good You've been to me

I'll count the joy come every battle

'Cause I know that's where You'll be

Another in the Fire —Hillsong United & TAYA

"I can't believe how strong you are."

Countless people told me this during Chris's cancer journey.

But here's the thing: I never felt alone. I never felt so strong. Even when our world was crumbling around us.

Instead, I had a powerful feeling that "there was another in the fire" with me and with our family during this trying time.

You've heard the story before. Shadrach, Meshack and Abednego refused to bow to the king, so he had them thrown into a fiery furnace. But when the king looked inside the fire, he saw four figures walking, not three. This freaked him out so he ordered his guards to pull them out of the fire. The three men were unscathed and their clothes didn't even smell like smoke. Check out Daniel 3 to read it for yourself.

I'm convinced that when we need God in a big way, he shows up in a big way.

In 2 Corinthians 12:9-10, we learn: "My grace is always more than enough for you, and My power finds its full expression through your weakness. So I will celebrate my weaknesses, for when I'm weak *I sense more deeply* the mighty power of Christ living in me. So I'm not defeated by my weakness, but delighted! For when I feel my weakness and endure mistreatment; when I'm surrounded with troubles on every side and face persecution because of my love for Christ, I am made yet stronger. For *my weakness becomes a portal to God's power.*"

These days, I fear less. When trouble comes, something tells me I've been through trouble before, and that God showed up in a big way. He will do it again. He promises to be with me in trouble. Psalm 91:15 says, "I will answer your cry for help every time you pray; and you will find and feel my presence even in your time of pressure and trouble."

I'm still looking for the scripture that tells me I'll never have any trouble. I haven't found that one yet. So be encouraged today! There truly is nothing to fear but fear itself. If you believe in God and reach out to Him he promises to be with you. This is the best news I've ever heard.

God's presence brought us through our biggest trial. Sometimes He sent his love through strangers; other times through wonderful friends and family. When we were weak, He sent us people who were strong. When we were in pain, He surrounded us with family and friends who made us feel loved and supported.

Even during those lonely moments when I paced the hospital hallway, waiting for my husband to endure yet another lumbar puncture, hoping against hope there was no cancer in his cerebrospinal fluid, I knew I wasn't alone. At those times I felt like I was being hugged with a warm blanket. So many tests, so many unknowns, yet I continually felt God's peace and presence.

And so I could give that confidence and love to my children, my husband, our families and friends. I could actually help those around me. It still amazes me that I had comfort to give.

Yes, God still works miracles, my friends. He has done it for me, and I know He will do it for you.

MY LETTER TO CANCER

"YOU NEVER KNOW HOW STRONG YOU ARE UNTIL BEING STRONG IS THE ONLY CHOICE YOU HAVE." —CAYLA MILLS

As I type these words, I can hardly see. Tears are streaming down my face as I think of our journey. I remember those who lost their fight and are with Jesus. We will see you again.

It's been seven years and counting since Chris's received his brand new bone marrow. We just returned from a visit to our oncologist, and as we were reminiscing about the cancer journey, he summed it up well.

"You've been to hell and back," he said.

That pretty much sums up what we went through as a family.

What do I want to say to cancer? I want to scream the ugliest things at it. I want to banish it to the far ends of existence. But yet, cancer has meant so much to me.

These words may help me explain.

Cancer is so limited....

It cannot cripple love

It cannot shatter hope

It cannot corrode faith

It cannot destroy peace

It cannot kill friendship

It cannot suppress memories

It cannot silence courage

It cannot invade the soul

It cannot steal eternal life

It cannot conquer the spirit.

What Cancer Cannot Do —Author unknown

It cannot cripple love.
Amen! In fact, it caused us to love more deeply.
So for that, cancer, I thank you. Cancer, you want to do nothing but cause pain and suffering and destruction in your wake, but you caused me and my family to love deeper and more fiercely. Sorry, not sorry, love wins once again.

It cannot shatter hope. It wants to. It will do everything in its power to shatter every last morsel of hope you didn't even know you had. But it cannot. On the contrary, it can make one hope beyond all hope. I once heard someone say, "get comfortable with the maybe." That is hope. Hope is maybe. Maybe I'll get better and maybe I'll beat this ugly disease. Maybe tomorrow will be better than today. Maybe they will find a cure. Maybe I will leave a legacy bigger than myself on this earth. Maybe I can love more deeply. Maybe the doctors will be wrong. Maybe the test will show smaller tumors. Maybe...and just maybe, if you are lucky or blessed enough to beat the cancer, you can give others hope. Hope which grew from an ugly disease.

See cancer, you make hope grow. You didn't destroy us.

It cannot corrode faith. Oh, it will try. Cancer can make you question everything, especially your faith. It's where the rubber meets the road. Here's the deal. Faith *is* that clench in the pit in your stomach That's right. You do it scared. That's true faith and something my husband taught me. You're okay with either outcome because you have faith. Faith in something and someone greater than yourself. You trust Him.

See, cancer? You made our faith grow beyond imagining. And now we know how to help someone else in trouble, to reach down for those who are struggling, to encourage them to hold onto their own faith.

It cannot destroy peace. It wants to! Yet peace isn't dependent on our circumstances. That's how I know cancer cannot destroy it. In fact, how you get back at cancer is you have peace no matter what. That's right! Peace in the face of ugly cancer.

Cancer, you helped us fight. You helped us fight with all we had, and in that fight we found an even greater peace.

It cannot kill friendship. Not true friendship, that's for sure. Cancer makes true friendships even stronger, tighter and more beautiful. Cancer caused us to see how many beautiful true friends we really had, and we had so many more than we thought.

Thank you for that, cancer. You lose again.

It cannot suppress memories. It can only make them sweeter, if that's what you choose to hang onto. Are there bad memories? I'd be lying if I said there weren't.

But cancer, you lose every time we choose to remember. To recall every single beautiful memory. You lose.

It cannot silence courage. That I can assure you. I watched my husband stare cancer dead in the face and go through excruciating treatments to beat it. If that isn't courage I don't know what is. Courage is every time you get a blood draw, a chemo treatment, a lumbar puncture, a bone marrow biopsy or any radiation treatment. Courage is waiting long days, hours and seconds for the results. Courage is throwing up and taking some more pills again.

Courage is every time a caregiver puts on a happy face, or even an angry one, and drives their loved one once again to the cancer clinic. Courage is the caregiver who holds the fort down; raises the kids, works or does any of the other support roles to help the cancer warrior continue the fight.

So cancer, don't even think about trying to silence our courage.

You can't and won't.

Courage is a twelve-year-old kid who has to step up to the pitcher's mound and throw in that pitch while his daddy is lying in a hospital bed trying to beat ugly cancer and it's hard to keep his mind on the so-called important game. It's when that same kid throws his helmet out of frustration and gets kicked out of the game by a compassionless umpire who has no idea what that kid is battling at home. That's courage. Courage is a twenty-one-year-old college student who walks straight out of school to come home and help his dad beat cancer.

Courage is a sixteen-year-old who keeps his shit together while watching his daddy waste away, not having any idea whether he will live or die, when he feels like he is going to fall apart.

I'll tell you what else courage looks like, it's an eighteen-year-old high school senior who has the choice to stay at home and finish up her high school career and do all the fun senior skip days and all the rest. That girl looks cancer dead in its face and says, "No, I want to be with my daddy." And she walks out the door and never looks back.

Cancer, you can never silence that kind of courage.

Courage is when your husband has to lie on his back naked and place his testicles on the so-called silver platter so they can direct the radiation directly to them, while his legs are bouncing so badly because he's lost all of his muscles from prednisone and cancer treatments.

Courage is taking a sales call in your apartment hallway, so the clients won't hear your kids laughing or fighting in the background, so you don't have to explain to them everything going on in your personal world. Or maybe you're in your car and you're taking another home loan application because your husband needs yet another blood transfusion but you also have to work to make money and keep health insurance. Or maybe you're working from the 6th floor of the cancer center in the super comfy reclining chairs waiting for a full day's worth of appointments and you have to be there with the cancer patient because this caregiving thing is a real job and it's not for the faint of heart. You have to be on your game.

I'll tell you the biggest courage of all. It's when your son-in-law has to watch his mama take her very last breath because her body has been so ravaged by leukemia and its treatments that it just cannot take any more, so she gives up her last breath and joins Jesus.

Cancer, you have absolutely no answer for that.

Cancer cannot invade the soul. Actually, I think it can, but you have to give it permission. I'll never give it that kind of power, and I hope you don't either. You have the choice to think what you will and allow the thoughts that consume your soul. You can't control your circumstances but you can control your attitude.

Cancer cannot steal eternal life. Ooh so good, and so true. Yes, it can take your earthly life, because none of us get out of this alive. There are a million ways to die. But cancer does NOT have the power to decide where you will spend eternity. It's only a vehicle to get you there. Anything that puts me face-to-face with my Lord?

I mean THANK YOU.

Based on everything we've experienced as a family, I would go out on a limb and say that cancer actually made eternal life even more obvious. The best way to live is when you know you're not going to be here forever. The Bible says, "Lord, teach me to number my days." It's a special thing to wake up each day saying, "Thank you that I woke up today."

Cancer, you taught us that each breath is a marvelous gift. Thank you for the reminder.

Cancer cannot conquer the spirit. Nope, that would be impossible. We carry the keys to that one. It is my belief that only we can conquer the spirit inside us. We may not get to choose what goes on with our bodies, but we get to choose whether our spirit is going to soar or give in.

Honestly, cancer, you can go f#@k yourself.

That's how this straight-laced mama and wife and now

grandma really feels. Cancer is the ugliest thing and it doesn't discriminate. You can be a pastor, an infant, any nationality, male or female, young or old. In a sense, cancer isn't the source of all of the destruction that cancer causes, Satan is. He is the master of destruction. The Bible says that he only comes to "steal, kill and destroy but that Jesus comes to give abundant life."

So to direct all my anger at cancer would be remiss. My anger is directed to Satan himself. He's the one who can go f#@k himself (sorry, mom).

As a Christian I know that God through Jesus his son has *already defeated* Satan. I believe sometimes when bad things happen, God didn't cause it but he allowed it. There's a difference. And I also believe that He is working "all things for my good."

So as much as I want to hate cancer and what it put us through as a family, I'm also grateful. I always tell people that I like the new Chris even better than before-cancer Chris.

He is once again my Superman, only now he is a superhero with empathy and patience. Thanks to cancer, he is an even better husband, father and grandpa than ever before.

IT IS FINISHED

"A MAN IS NOT FINISHED WHEN HE IS DEFEATED. HE IS FINISHED WHEN HE QUITS."

You know by now that our family loves worship music. And you know how much we love to hear our daughter Joya sing. Here is one of her favorite songs. And after our cancer journey together, every word has new meaning for the Harper family.

Seems like all I can see was the struggle

Haunted by ghosts that lived in my past

Bound up in shackles of all my failures

Wondering how long is this gonna last

Then You look at this prisoner and say to me "son

Stop fighting a fight that's already been won"

I am redeemed, You set me free

So I'll shake off these heavy chains

And wipe away every stain now I'm not who I used to be

I am redeemed

I'm redeemed

All my life I have been called unworthy
Named by the voice of my shame and regret
But when I hear You whisper, "Child lift up your head"
I remember oh God, You're not done with me yet

I am redeemed, You set me free
So I'll shake off these heavy chains
And wipe away every stain now I'm not who I used to be
Because I don't have to be the old man inside of me
'Cause his day is long dead and gone
Because I've got a new name, a new life I'm not the same
And a hope that will carry me home

I am redeemed, You set me free
So I'll shake off these heavy chains
And wipe away every stain now I'm not who I used to be

I am redeemed, You set me free
So I'll shake off these heavy chains
And wipe away every stain now I'm not who I used to be

Oh God I'm not who I used to be
Jesus I'm not who I used to be

'Cause I am redeemed
Thank God, redeemed

Redeemed —Big Daddy Weave

In John 19:30, Jesus said, "It is finished!" Then He bowed His head and surrendered His spirit to God.

At the end of the day, all that matters is what Jesus did for us. Whenever I complain to Chris about something or other, he always has a gentle reminder.

"Yes, but look at what Jesus did for us," he says. "What he went through. No matter what you ever go through it would never come close to what Jesus did."

It is finished means there is nothing more to add. The work is complete. You, too, can have this assurance in your spiritual self, knowing that God's work is complete in you.

John 3:16 -17 says, "This is how much God loved the world: He gave his one and only, unique Son as a gift. So now everyone who believes in him will never perish but experience everlasting life. God did not send his Son into the world to judge and condemn the world, but to be its Saviour and rescue it."

Be assured of this truth. Whether your time comes today, or 100 years from now, you can live the rest of your life with hope in your heart. Not only is God with you on earth, He is also ready to receive you when you die.

I hope and pray that you can feel Him by your side.

HARPERS HOUSE
OF HOPE

"SHE IS CLOTHED IN STRENGTH AND DIGNITY AND SHE
LAUGHS WITHOUT FEAR OF THE FUTURE."

—PROVERBS 31:25

And now, I want you to picture one more thing.
Remember the prophecy?

"I keep seeing this vacation home..... (there it is). I don't see the whole picture, but there is treasure in it. There are generational blessings associated with this. I don't see the whole picture but whatever it is if you can hold onto it. I see treasure chests all around it. God has placed favor on your life. Keep trusting God. Push past every obstacle. The Lord doesn't want you to let go of memories for the sake of anything else. Keep memories alive. They are your most valuable asset. *I see this house. I don't know if you own it, or if you are going to buy it or if it's in the family. It might be a vacation property? Focus on building memories and keeping them alive.* There are generational blessings coming down from previous generations and generational blessings you will pass on."

My friends, we don't know where our story will end, but we did just buy a home on a lake in a beautiful place. It's a place beyond our dreams. We want to share this place with our family and friends and people like cancer families who have been

175

through a lot.

We don't know how or when or what that will look like, but we are going to make a ton of memories, God willing, and share this blessing with as many people as we can.

Together, let's spread the hope that keeps us going through good times and bad.

Now that's a legacy worth living for.

PHOTOS

Chris and Shelley Harper prior to their cancer journey.

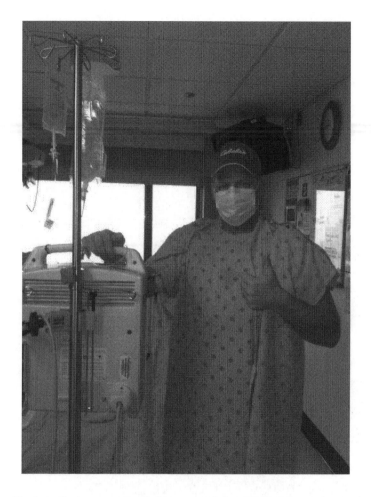

Chris's first round of chemo. Always the thumbs up!

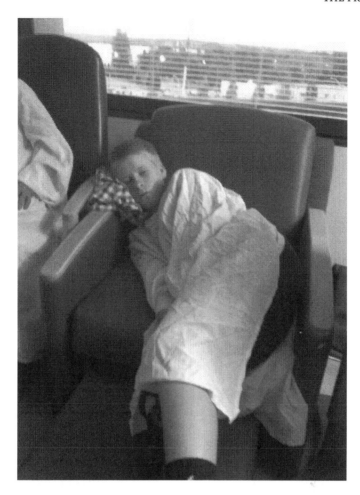

Getting tired the day of the bone marrow transplant.

Josh and Jordan with Chris and his brother Keith.

Head shaving party hair finally started coming out.

The boys shaved their heads in solidarity.

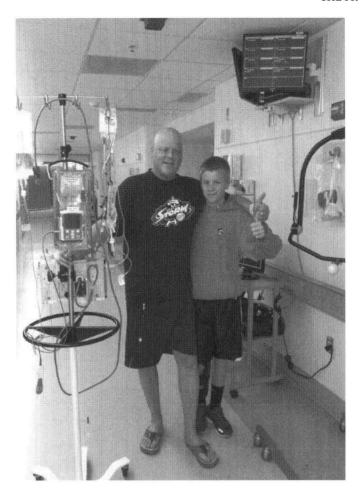

Jared "walking laps" with Dad.

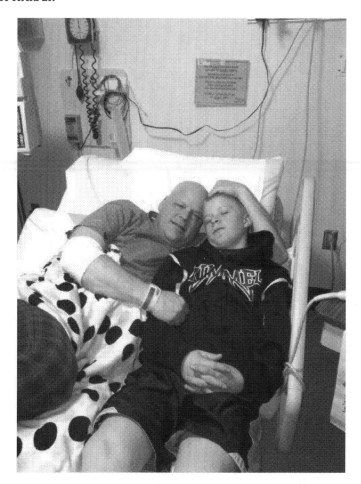

More snuggle time with Dad in the hospital.

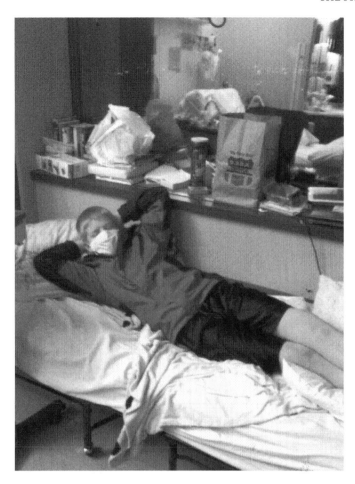

Jared getting tired from visiting Dad.

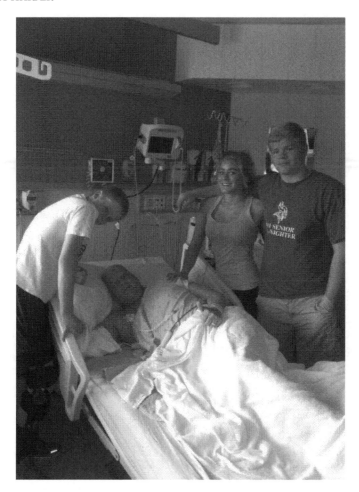

More time with Dad in the hospital.

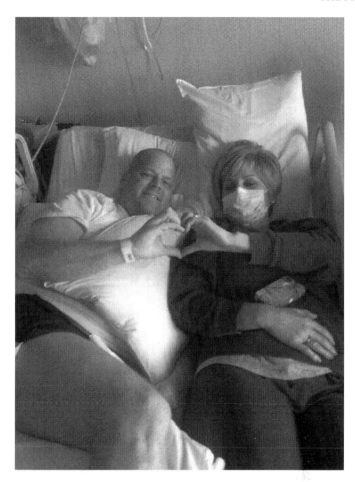

Chris and Shelley had plenty of snuggle time.

"Cheating" and having crab buffet, but oh so happy!

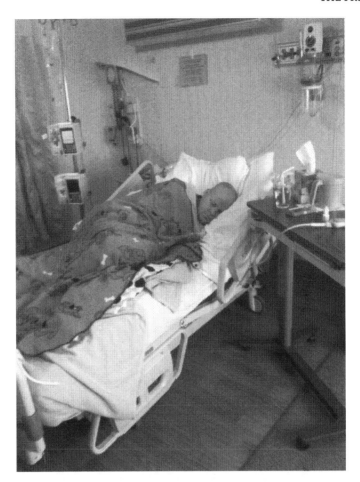

Watching my man sleep for hours on end.

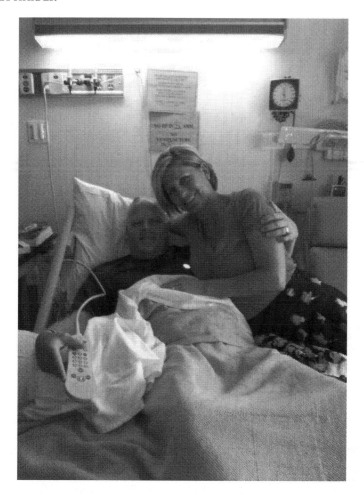

Visiting Chris in the hospital on Mother's Day.

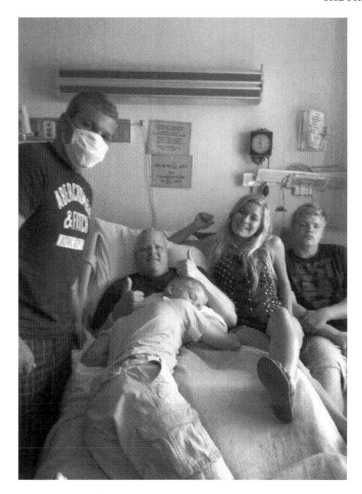

All the kids visiting Dad in the hospital again.

Our "camping trip" from hell.

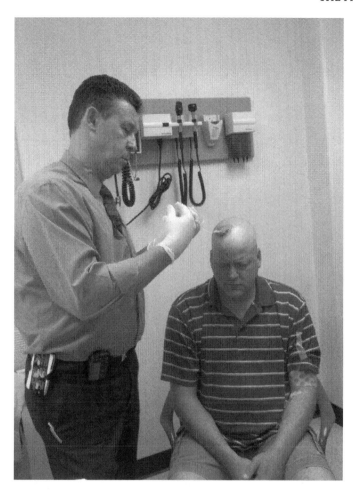

Chris's doctor administering brain chemo.

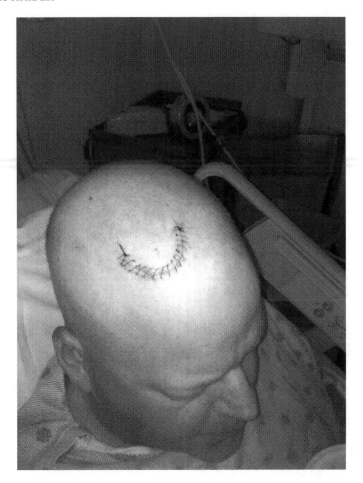

Brain surgery with the Ommaya port.

Victory! Chris retrieved his trail cam
right after having brain surgery.

One eye shut, but always the thumbs up!

Chris and Shelley's new shared "birthday."

All four of the kids visiting Dad the day of his transplant.

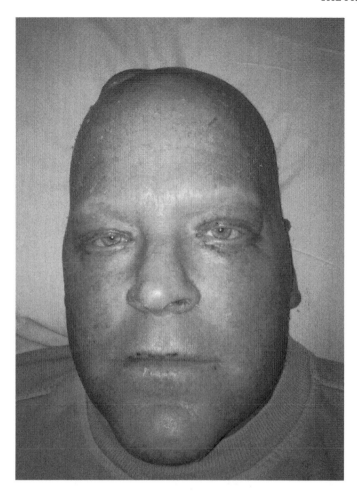

The face of GVHD.

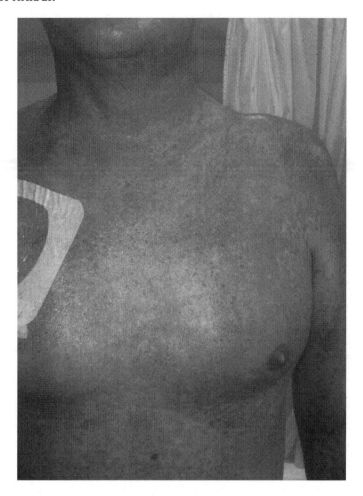

GVHD skin.

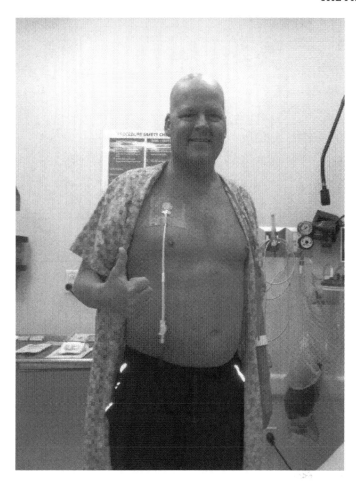

Getting his Hickman removed so he could go home.

A rare outing to the park with the kids after transplant.

Family picture after recovery, left to right:
Shelley, Jared, Joya, Jordan, Chris and Josh.

Joya and Shelley getting on the registry at bethematch.org

Yes, there is definitely laughter after cancer!

EPILOGUE

One night I dreamed a dream.

As I was walking along the beach with my Lord.

Across the dark sky flashed scenes from my life.

For each scene, I noticed two sets of footprints in the sand, One belonging to me and one to my Lord.

After the last scene of my life flashed before me, I looked back at the footprints in the sand.

I noticed that at many times along the path of my life, especially at the very lowest and saddest times, there was only one set of footprints.

This really troubled me, so I asked the Lord about it.

"Lord, you said once I decided to follow you, You'd walk with me all the way.

But I noticed that during the saddest and most troublesome times of my life, there was only one set of footprints.

I don't understand why, when I needed You the most, You would leave me."

He whispered, "My precious child, I love you and will never leave you Never, ever, during your trials and testings.

When you saw only one set of footprints, It was then that I carried you." —*Footprints in the Sand*

ACKNOWLEDGEMENT

I would like to thank Jim Morrison for referring an editor to me! I would like to thank my editor David Kilmer for taking our story and giving it wings! I can't thank him enough for his encouragement, expertise and knowledge of this process. You are one of my angels. To my mom, thank you for asking me hundreds of times how my book was coming! (when it wasn't making any progress) your encouragement kept me pushing forward. To Chris and the kids, thank you for your encouragement to write the book and for listening to me talk about it over and over again. Thanks for living this story with me; we will forever have this in common. Thanks for believing in me.

ABOUT THE AUTHOR

Shelley Harper

I was born and raised in the beautiful state of Colorado and grew up hiking and riding horses in the high mountains. I've been married to my husband Chris for 30 years and we have raised four wonderful children. We recently welcomed  our first grandson and granddaughter. I am a loan officer and a writer living in gorgeous Northern Idaho. I am passionate about helping women see their full potential and doing anything I can to support and inspire cancer patients, their caregivers and their families. Together with my husband who is a leukemia survivor, our mission is to bring hope to those suffering. When not working I enjoy hanging out with my family, playing on the lake, hiking, traveling, going to concerts, reading and playing with my dog and five granddogs.

Made in the USA
Monee, IL
14 April 2021